C000070674

My National Service (1955 – 1957)

The Making of a Man

Also by Brian Holdich

My Indian Journey

India Revisited

The 2001 New York City Marathon

Stanground Boy
(Yesterday in Poems)

The Man from the PRU

The Torchbearers
(The Olympic Torch in Peterborough)

My National Service (1955 – 1957)

The Making of a Man

Brian Holdich

Foreword by
Major (Rtd) Reverend Neil Knox

Publications

Copyright ©2019 by Brian Holdich
Revised Edition ©March 2023 by Brian Holdich

All rights reserved. No part of this publication may be reproduced, stored in a retrieval system, or transmitted in any form or by any means—for example, electronic, photocopy, recording—without the prior written permission of the publisher. The only exception is brief quotations in printed reviews.

British Library Cataloguing-in-Publication Data.
A catalogue record for this book is available from The British Library.

ISBN: 978-0-9956231-2-5 (Paperback)
ISBN: 978-1-913579-62-3 (E-Publication)

Publisher: Ladey Adey Publications, 1 Ermine Street, Ancaster, Lincolnshire, UK.

Cover Picture by Abbirose Adey, Ladey Adey Publications.

Author address is Market Deeping, Peterborough, UK.

Royalties collected from the sale of this book will go to charity which include the St Guthlac's Church in Market Deeping.

Dedication

*I dedicate this book to two brothers
who fought in the First World War,
one being my father Tom,
who survived the horrors of trench warfare
and the other, his younger brother Charles,
aged 19, who never returned home.*

Travelling 28,000 miles in 2 years

Brian's Travels during his National Service

Outward Journey	Miles
Southampton to Gibraltar	1,356.4
Gibraltar to Port Said	2,789.3
Port Said to Mukalla (Aden)	2,101.2
Mukalla to Sri Lanka	2,190.0
Sri Lanka to Singapore	1,650.0
Singapore to Hong Kong	1,862.0
Sub Total	11,948.9 miles
Return Journey	Miles
Hong Kong to Singapore	1,862.0
Singapore to Sri Lanka	1,650.0
Sri Lanka to Mukalla	2,190.0
Mukalla to Zanzibar	1,372.0
Zanzibar to Cape Town	2,327.0
Cape Town to Freetown	3,594.0
Freetown to Southampton	2,997.9
Sub Total	15,992.9 miles
Total miles (not including Germany, Holland and other smaller destinations)	27,941.8 miles

Acknowledgements

To the Reverend Neil Knox, who kindly wrote the foreword for this book. He was a Regular soldier in the British Army for many years. He served in Northern Ireland during all the troubles there, achieving the rank of Major. We met when Neil was a curate at the St Guthlac's Church in Market Deeping where he became extremely popular.

I must give my heartfelt thanks to Caron Romaine who typed the original manuscript of this book. I must have annoyed her at times with constant alterations, but she never showed any annoyance with me and I'll always be grateful for that.

I have to thank an unknown soldier who, like me, was in B Company of the Essex Regiment in Hong Kong. He gave me all the small photographs used in this book. In all honesty, I have completely forgotten his name and I would personally loved to have thanked him.

The wise words of my good friend Ted Roberts, who was in the RAF during the Second World War. He would often give me invaluable information concerning this particular war.

Another good friend, my next door neighbour, Geoff Chambers. Geoff worked out the total number of miles I travelled during my two years in the Army, exactly 28,000 miles.

Brian Holdich May 2019.

About the Author

Brian Holdich was born in Stanground, Peterborough in 1935 when after attending Stamford School he started an apprenticeship in Electrical Engineering. He was then called up in 1955 to serve his two years National Service where he spent the majority of his time in the British Army in Hong Kong. Here he played plenty of football but unfortunately no cricket. It was in the early days in the army that he took up boxing again, just to prove a point and he had some success.

On being demobbed in February 1957 he eventually joined the Prudential as 'The Man from the Pru' where he found happiness in a well loved occupation.

In retirement he can often be found watching his old club, Market Deeping Cricket Club and in his late forties he became a walker when he completed fourteen marathons. When his last marathon 'The New York City Marathon', which proved to be really tough and he suffered a badly damaged ankle which put an end to his marathon walking. Another enjoyment for Brian was when he discovered the joy of writing having been the author with this book being his seventh and last book.

It was due to his charity work that he was nominated to be a Torchbearer on 3rd July 2012 when he carried the Olympic Torch through the crowded streets of his home city of Peterborough.

Brian had been married to Kathleen for fifty eight years until they had to say goodbye when she passed away in 2020. They have a daughter and a son, three grandchildren and three great grandchildren.

Contents

National Service

The First World War brought death and destruction on a monumental scale prompting people to remark, *"Never again"*. Yet, a mere 21 years after Armistice Day, the Second World War was to happen again against the old enemy, Germany.

It was then after the Second World War that the British Government brought in a National Service being formed across the whole of Great Britain involving thousands of young men. At the age of 18 they would be required to serve two years National Service in Her Majesty's Forces.

This would mean that Great Britain would be more prepared in the event of another World War than it had ever been before.

Evidently NATO (North Atlantic Treaty Organisation) was formed initially involving 12 founding countries. This is now 29 countries which include Great Britain, America and many other countries across the world with the premise that if any of these nations were attacked by a hostile enemy then NATO would act in the appropriate forceful manner, despite the fear of another World War, which fortunately has never materialised.

To make the world a much safer place it meant that many of Great Britain's National Service soldiers would invariably be sent abroad soon after their army training had finished. In order to keep the peace in many countries across the world; Hong Kong, India, Singapore, Cyprus, Malta, Malaya and Yemen to name just a few countries where hostilities had already broken out and not forgetting Germany where since the end of the Second World War many British soldiers were still required but not any more.

There was a great need that British soldiers would always be needed somewhere in the world. So here was I about to become a National Service soldier and I felt I was well up for the task by being fit and in good health. So I had no real fears whatsoever on leaving civilian life, well maybe just slightly nervous, but I rather stupidly believed that my army training would be a mere formality. I soon realised how wrong I could possibly be!

Foreword

You will often hear people lament the ending of conscription in 1960 to National Service believing it would perhaps help improve the fabric of our society today. Certainly, for those who completed National Service, it provided an opportunity to encounter and travel far beyond the normal horizon open to many young men at the time. Brian's book strikingly captures the experience of a 19-year old young man, from the suburbs of industrial Peterborough, on National Service in the mid 1950s.

In his account, we journey with him on a two year round-the-world adventure where he outlines his hopes for the experience as well as capturing the highs and lows that transpire in his 28,000 miles of travel. From the inevitable shock of basic training, where men from wide socio-economic backgrounds are seemingly arbitrarily thrown together in the transition process from civilian to soldier, we see how these life-long friendships, unique to the military environment, are forged. He paints a vivid picture of the arduous voyage on an ageing troopship from Southampton, through the Mediterranean and Suez Canal, before reaching his destination of Hong Kong where he would remain for 14 months. In so doing, we are given a window to images from a bygone era from a spotlessly clean Mediterranean to arriving in the embryonic metropolis of Hong Kong.

From humorous encounters and experiences in a colonial Hong Kong, spanning ballroom dancing to field exercises, whilst protecting the border in the New Territories only a stone's throw from the Chinese town of Shenzhen, we then head back to Great Britain on a return journey which, touched the emerging Suez Crisis necessitating a re-route home around the Cape of South Africa calling in at Zanzibar and apartheid Cape Town.

This book is so much more than a diary account of what took place over Brian's two years of National Service in the 1950s; this is a story about how the experience touched, shaped and *'made'* the man. In his own words;

"I can remember it far more than any other two years of my entire life... it was the making of me".

Major (Retired) Reverend Neil Knox

Introduction

I first thought about writing this book 23 years ago, after I was made redundant from The Prudential. At that time, I rather reluctantly came to the conclusion that it was a far too arduous a venture for me to even contemplate. One big fear was whether I would find a publisher willing to publish my work. So, I shelved the idea: hoping to come back to it at another time; hoping that my memory would hold and that dementia would not strike. If it did, all my National Service memories would disappear completely. So I had to move quickly.

I decided to undertake the task of writing about my National Service days as I continue to surprise myself with how much I remember from those 'never to be forgotten' days, now over sixty years ago. Looking back to that time, I realise that my time in the army was the pinnacle of my teenage years, which I'm sure I'll never forget. Is it any wonder then, that I can recall what happened at that time most clearly. Yet, things that happened a few months, or even a few weeks ago I've drawn a blank! The fear of dementia as we get older is never far away and I believe writing this book has helped me enormously revealing the answers to difficult questions that have been stored away somewhere in my brain. I'm so grateful that my memory is still good.

Conscription or National Service as it was more commonly known had one willing occupant who was actually looking forward to serving in Her Majesty's Forces. The reason for this was that I wanted to travel and see as much of the world as I possibly could. Previously, I had been turned down in my application to join the REME. Although, I wasn't too disappointed I felt I stood a better chance of achieving what had became an ambition with National Service.

I learned that the 2nd Battalion, the Northampton-shire Regiment were serving in the Far East in Hong Kong, and being born and bred in this county I thought I stood a good chance of getting in, which indeed, proved to be the case. However, never in my wildest dreams did I ever envisage that on leaving Great Britain for Hong Kong I would travel literally thousands of miles by ship and due to a diversion, even more on the return sea voyage home.

"What was National Service, Granddad?"

It was during my two year's National Service that I visited eight countries in all, by sailing on some of the greatest seas of the world. Now, years later I can still look back on the ambition I had at 19 years of age, and realise that I was able to complete such a goal by sailing on three Troop carrier ships.

I'm sure that National Service in my time (1955-1957) was regarded by some, as a sort of institution albeit used for a very good purpose. Today, it's almost forgotten and this was brought to mind when my grandson, Daniel Woods, in all innocence asked,

"What was National Service, Granddad?"

I thought I have to write about this as many of the younger generation have never heard of National Service, it has become part of the history books and mentioned briefly within National Armed Forces Day. My hope is that this book will be taken seriously and will explain to young people in their teens the full meaning of National service which for me, to delve back over 60 years has been an absolute delight.

Brian Holdich
(June 2019)

Since the publication of this book, I have felt the need to produce a revised edition, adding a few remnants of memory that I omitted in the original version. When the pandemic, and consequently lockdown, struck the world in 2020, I was unable to sell the book in my usual way – person to person – hopefully I can get back to it now. One consolation during this time is the book received numerous five-star ratings on Amazon. If you enjoyed the book, please add your own review.

Brian Holdich
(March 2023)

"We do not seek peace in order to be at war,
but we go to war that we may have peace.
Be peaceful, therefore, in warring,
so that you may vanquish those
whom you war against, and
bring them to the prosperity of peace."

St Augustine

1

Quebec Barracks

When I received my call-up papers in February 1955, my two year National Service with the 1st Battalion of the Northamptonshire Regiment was about to begin. I should have joined a year earlier but because I was serving an apprenticeship at Peterborough Power Station I was deferred for a year. So when I actually enlisted into the British Army I was enthusiastic and looked forward to my two year National Service. I certainly didn't want to be deferred for another year.

The excitement of how I felt then, that I would be serving my country in Hong Kong, was very special indeed. As the 2nd Battalion of the Northamptonshire Regiment was stationed there, this would be a great opportunity of seeing as much of the world as possible. Was it any wonder then that I was full of optimism and hope with what my two year National Service could offer me? My work colleagues who had already been in the Forces had told me,

"Don't be rebellious in any way as the Army will soon sort you out!"

My two year National Service was to start on the 17th February 1955, where at the age of 19, I had to report to Quebec Barracks, which were located in Northampton. I caught a train, nice and early, from Peterborough and then found myself in the company of two young men whom I had befriended that morning, as they had also been called up. On arriving at Northampton Railway Station, it was plainly obvious to see other young men who were also going to sign on at Quebec Barracks. Then, an army truck arrived to take all of us to our final destination and my two year National Service was about to begin. Little did I realise, this would be the start of a visit to eight different countries in all and I would travel halfway across the world serving the Queen and my country.

The platoon I was about to join, in the Northamptonshire Regiment, was the Somme Platoon in B Company. The name of the Somme originates from the Battle of the Somme, in the First World War. Here the Northamptonshire Regiment and other regiments of the British Army suffered the most appalling losses imaginable. Thousands upon thousands lost their lives after war was declared with Germany in 1914.

Young men, throughout Great Britain, willingly left their homes and families in the expectation that the war would be over in a few months. Horrifyingly, it dragged on for four, long years. I wondered, How on earth did my father manage to survive in those ghastly trenches? I will never know.

He was injured twice and he spent a considerable amount of time in an army hospital. Like a lot of other British soldiers he never mentioned anything about the First World War. He preferred to block it out of his memory completely. Not so fortunate was my father's youngest brother Charles, who at the age of 19, lost his life to a sniper's bullet. Evidently, his death was instantaneous and he apparently didn't suffer unduly. I have more recently learned that the word instantaneous on a death report did not always mean a quick death. Simply, the word was used to lessen the impact of suffering for the close family, whether wife or parent, reading the dreadful news on such a tragic occurrence.

Recruits B Company of the 1st Battalion, Northamptonshire Regiment (1955).
Just before the start of the Passing Out Parade.
Private Holdich is standing top row fourth from the left.

2

The Platoon Sergeant

When that lorry load of new recruits arrived that day at Quebec Barracks, it was most evident that many other young men had also received their call-up papers making a total of about 100 men in all. On arriving at the barracks my feet hardly touched the ground as I was being pushed from pillar to post, from one barrack room to another barrack room. There was no let-up whatsoever, as we were being kitted out with, literally, arms full of army clothes, notably; uniforms, denims, boots, underwear and numerous other essential parts of army clothing. Not forgetting the bedding, including a heavy mattress. I found it extremely difficult to carry everything at once while looking for the appropriate barrack room that I would be living in during my initial training (which I eventually found, thank goodness!).

It was then a mad dash to get a haircut as I had been told my hair was too long. And to think, I had already had a civilian haircut just a few days before! My army haircut looked as though I had been scalped. After all this, we were told to get to the cookhouse, which seemed a good idea as some of us had hardly eaten that day. Luckily, we made it just in time before it was closed for the day. This situation was far from ideal as some of the recruits were already starting to grumble which was natural in view of the circumstances. After a few more busy hours we were finally allowed to go to our allocated barrack rooms where we flopped to our beds in exhaustion.

There were a total of sixteen beds in each barrack room with a big heated stove in the centre to keep us warm on cold February nights. It was during all that rushing about that I met our Platoon Sergeant, whose name was Davis. He was hardly going to replace my mother as he had the air of being full of his own importance and seemed to have a permanent smirk on his face. I've heard it said that one should never judge anyone on first impressions, which can be misleading, but I have to be honest, my first impression of the man was not good at all and I was hardly in awe of him, but I kept my thoughts to myself, as the discipline during training would be tough. I obviously didn't want to rock the boat by getting on the wrong side of him. I had just got to knuckle down and accept what came my way.

I also knew that the nine weeks of initial training could easily be the worst part of my two years of National Service and that in a few days time we would start rehearsing drill, known as square bashing, on the square everyday. This was in preparation for the Passing Out Parade, which would be held on a Saturday afternoon at the end of April. All the drill work would mean endless hours of repetition, I was sure it would get very boring. I quickly learned that if I didn't try to enjoy those two years in front of me then it could be a very long time indeed, but all this square bashing would be a test of one's character which would be very much a big part of the training to become a British infantry soldier.

One of the things that intrigued me in those early days of National Service was this: How would people of; entirely different backgrounds; different standards of education; different religions and different upbringing, all mix together? All these different individuals had to share a barrack room together and had never set eyes on one another before. Could this situation create a strained relationship in the barrack room? How would the Oxbridge University student who was educated at a public school, from an elite background, cope finding that in the bed next to him was a boy of the same age who came from an entirely different background, born in the poorest part of a big city, where he hardly ever attended school? How could these so different human beings have anything in common with each other? Who would make the first move? Or would they completely ignore one another? I have seen this situation myself in the barrack room and it became a most interesting predicament. The two boys concerned, tolerated each other without ever falling out, and that was as far as they were prepared to go. I've known similar situations where a good relationship emerged.

When in War time one could become an officer and the other a foot soldier yet despite differences, they would hopefully defeat the enemy. It proved comradeship in the battlefield mattered the most whatever one's social status might be.

"Discipline is the soul of an army.
It makes small numbers formidable;
procures success to the weak,
and esteem to all."

George Washington.

3

It was all Bull

To start every morning at the 6am Reveille, Corporal Waller, our Platoon Corporal, would go berserk on bursting into our barrack room bellowing out, *"Wakey, wakey, rise and shine!"* as loud as he possibly could by nearly pulling us out of our beds. This unwanted ritual was repeated every single morning, apart from Sunday, of our nine weeks initial training informing everyone in no uncertain manner that we had to wash, shave and dress in double quick time, in order to make it for breakfast.

After a hurried breakfast we would be standing at the side of our beds waiting for the morning kit inspection. This could be a personal embarrassment, if one's clothing wasn't up to the required standard. We would be warned and if it was repeated again we could be put on a charge. The kit inspection team usually consisted of Sergeant Davis and Corporal Waller and once a week the Platoon Officer, Lieutenant Evans-Evans. (The Lieutenant incidentally came from Peterborough. Of whom I have to report no favours were ever given.)

The morning kit inspection was not just on what we were wearing but literally everything owned by the army that was in our own possession. It had to be immaculately clean and if it was found with the slightest speck of dirt or dust there would be trouble. All the items of clothing would be displayed; having everything laid out, every morning, on our beds. Also, the blankets from the bed would be laid square at the pillow end in traditional army fashion. It was most noticeable that Sergeant Davis would be most attentive when he was inspecting all the items spread out on my bed.

In addition, under intense inspection was a soldier's rifle; this was a soldier's pride, and indeed a privilege, to have in his custody. A rifle is often known as an infantryman's best friend.

When inspected, the rifle would have to be in a dustless condition. Extra special attention would be concentrated on the barrel of the rifle, which had to be clean at all times. During wartime, the rifle would never leave a soldiers' side and is handled with great care and affection. If it was not totally clean, it would be absolutely useless on the battlefield and would be unable to fire a single shot.

There really was in training lots of bull which made us grumble at times as all of us recruits would be expected to maintain the high standards set by the army. I'm sure that over sixty years ago we all hoped to aspire to these standards and if all the discipline were to make us more independent then hopefully we could become better soldiers. The bull continued with even more bull as I can recall; the barrack room floor was polished relentlessly by a big buff machine, where we took it in turns to either push it or pull it. Every day, windows inside the barrack room along with the inside of the big entrance door was meticulously cleaned, there was no let up. If after all that bull, it was found that the odd cobweb was still about, it really was an insult of scandalous proportion. If cobwebs could still be seen, it would be enough for one such platoon sergeant to have a heart attack, namely Sergeant Davis (but I wouldn't wish that on him).

I do not recall any soldier crying in his bed at night during training, due to unhappiness, but I recall one soldier seemed near to breaking down. Only the friendship of fellow soldiers helped and kept him going. Those of a nervous disposition who hardly opened their mouths and suffered inwardly were those I pitied.

A young soldier's unhappiness during National Service, which was often his first time away from home, may have stemmed from missing his mother - especially if he shared a strong, loving relationship. Often on the battlefield the dying thoughts of a young soldier may have been of his mother, and he may have murmured her name – a poignant thought and not one of which to be ashamed.

The author (on left) with his best friend Les.
If I look smarter than him it was because I had just
come off guard duty at the Fanling Army Camp.

4

Best of Friends

It has been said many times that friendships made in the Forces are some of the best friendships one is ever likely to make. I personally can vouch for this, as the friendship I had with Les Knight, who came from Raunds in Northamptonshire, was one such friendship. This happened because of the close proximity of two such soldiers in Her Majesties Forces, which meant we stuck together like glue and we became firm friends, always there for each other. Being thousands of miles from home, to have that special friend whom one could trust was extraordinary. Yet, in many respects we were very different individuals indeed. Much of my life has been involved with the sports I played. You name it I have done it (or should I say, tried it) but was never good enough to make it. Les was inclined not to be the sporting type but he enjoyed fishing and loved his pigeons. It wouldn't do for all of us human beings to be the same in this world and Les was certainly different in that respect.

What a character he was and we had many a good laugh. He could tell a good yarn to anyone, or even groups of people, who were prepared to listen to him. He would write to his girlfriend every day and he had already asked me to be Best Man at his wedding when he was demobbed.

When I married Kathleen in Chester a few years later he was one of the first guests I wanted at the wedding. We kept in touch for many years but lost contact as we both moved house a few times.

Then, one Christmas his daughter telephoned me to invite Kathleen and me to see him. *"You must come and see him, Brian, as he is not at all well and he is forever talking about you and his army days."*

On visiting Les, he seemed an entirely different person to the man I knew. He had been a bricklayer and a barrel load of bricks fell on him and he hadn't worked since. Then about twelve years ago again at Christmas, a very trembling and tired voice spoke on the telephone informing me that he had cancer and it was evident I was losing a great friend, who had helped me throughout my army career. As I write, my eyes are swelling somewhat,

"Sleep well my old friend until we meet again. I will never forget you."

5

An Infantry Soldier (Square Bashing)

I was in Somme Platoon B Company and there were two other platoons in B Company of which all the recruits hoped to be fully-fledged soldiers one day. Everyday after breakfast, and the daily kit inspection, we would be out on the Square going through the usual motions of drill, which we were required to do under the leadership of Sergeant Davis.

He would not tolerate any laziness and required from everyone the highest possible standards. To be second best was not for him. I shall always recall one of his classic comments. One day, we were struggling to get everything together properly when he remarked, "If you broke your mother's heart when you left her, you certainly won't break mine". He really was a tough taskmaster and sometimes I felt that I was on some sort of apprenticeship as he was so thorough in his training of us to become good soldiers. This hopefully would stand us in good stead when we joined the 2nd Battalion of the

Northamptonshire Regiment in Hong Kong.

As time progressed by, I began to realise that all the square bashing was very much an ingredient of being in the infantry. Just occasionally I might have cast my mind back, that if I had been accepted into the REME I would not necessarily have been involved with the constant square bashing. In the REME I would at least be working in electrical engineering (which I was being trained for in my civilian life) but I have to write that if I had joined the REME I would have missed out on the glorious opportunity of achieving my ambition, serving the British Army abroad. This undoubtedly would have been a major disappointment, as more than ever I wanted to travel and see the world. I knew I would never get this opportunity in my civilian working life.

It was not all square bashing and it was a relief and a most enjoyable experience to try something else. I did enjoy testing my skills on the rifle range. We would indulge ourselves in whether we could produce a good shot or not. It was imperative in the infantry, as a rifleman in the British Army, that on pulling the trigger we became a reasonable shot and at least maintain this (unfortunately we didn't always hit the bullseye) but it really was a delight trying.

It was noticeable that some of our platoon were naturals at using a rifle, while others were all over the place. I found that the more practice I had the better I became and that applied to the others also. What really surprised me was that we didn't visit the rifle range more often, especially in view of the fact that we would be leaving soon for Hong Kong and ultimately trying to keep the peace with neighbouring China.

Usually when war is declared anywhere in the world, it is likely the infantry will be the first involved. If we arrived in Hong Kong and there was immediate trouble with China, I knew that all the new recruits would have benefited considerably by more practice on the rifle range.

The throwing of a live hand grenade can be highly dangerous, particularly when the pin on the grenade has been removed. If the grenade is thrown and at that moment it slips out of one's hand, it means that your own soldiers could be endangered as it drops to the ground. It will undoubtedly cause an explosion. By far the safest way of delivering a live hand grenade is to lob it from the hand with an over arm action (not unlike a cricketer bowling a cricket ball). Before a hand grenade is delivered one must know how far away the actual target is. Then on delivering the live hand grenade one must immediately drop to the ground, to protect oneself from a massive explosion. Even in practice we were made well aware of the dangers of holding a live hand grenade, as many major accidents with live hand grenades have proved to be very costly to one's own soldiers. (I can only describe holding a live hand grenade is like holding a newborn baby for the first time, as one should never drop it.)

"None but an armed nation can dispense with a standing army. To keep ours armed and disciplined is therefore at all times important."

Thomas Jefferson.

6

Bayonet Practice

I know that we only practiced bayonet fighting and I felt most uncomfortable at the thought of having to take part in something as hideous as bayonet combat. First watching, and then practicing, such a frightful and grisly activity. I emphasize my intense dislike, when along with the other recruits partaking in this barbaric ritual killing of a fellow human we pretended we were fighting in the trenches.

A dummy figure representing the human body was placed in front of us. As we proceeded to attack the enemy, we were taught to run with a bayonet fixed to the barrel end of the rifle, encouraged to shout an obscene word and then thrust the sharp bayonet into the dummy's belly. This left me feeling completely cold and ill at ease with myself.

Whenever we were required to do bayonet practice I would invariably think of my father Tom, who in his early twenties, and his younger brother, Charles, nearly nineteen years of age, both volunteering in the First World War. Both fought in the trenches, and one never returned home. It is Charles who was involved with close bayonet fighting against German soldiers. He received a nasty bayonet wound to his hand and was immediately sent home to Cambridge Hospital, where he recuperated. Can we begin to imagine the pressure that boy was under, when in hospital recovering, and knowing full well he would be returned to the hell hole that was the front line in the trenches again? He may have, in his inner thoughts, considered doing a runner and desert the army, but he'd then be accused of cowardice. Like a lot of soldiers he just couldn't do such a thing. After six weeks, my Uncle Charlie fully recovered and returned to the front only to be killed on 4th June 1916.

It had always been an ambition of mine to locate Charles' grave in Moroc, France. About twelve years ago, I travelled there with my brother Gordon and our wives. We found his gravestone with the Holdich name on it, which nearly reduced us to tears. Will mankind ever learn? I hope I have given enough reason why I detested the practice of bayonet fighting.

Another relative, who served in the great war had the unenviable job of collecting the dead from the battlefield. This changed him and affected his mind resulting in early demobilisation. On arriving home, his wife hardly recognised him. They later divorced unable to reconcile his mental instability - just one of the many repercussion of war.

During initial training, I would often think of British soldiers, like my dad and my uncle, who fought in WWI. They fought in the trenches contending with the bitterly cold temperatures; snow, rain and mud up to their knees. I cannot in all honesty think of a worst place to die.

7

Put on a Charge

What I can remember most vividly is when I was put on charge and sentenced to two days with 'jankers'. The punishment for being over two hours late on returning to Quebec Barracks after going to the pictures one evening in Northampton. A social evening had been arranged where local Northampton girls were invited to a dance purely for the benefit of all the soldiers. Some of the recruits were swarming all over these girls like bees and as I'd got no commitment with regard to a girlfriend back home

So, it was out of curiosity when I was persuaded by some of the lads form our Barracks to attend this dance. I never thought for one single moment that I would land myself in serious trouble by being put on a charge! I'd been in the Army only a few weeks and this was the last thing I wanted.

What a way to start my two years National Service. I was to experience the full force of Army discipline. I very much regretted attending that dance as I had to pay the consequences of my actions, which I believe was not necessarily my fault as the hierarchy in the army from corporal upwards just didn't seem to believe me. I will now once more tell the truth and nothing but the truth about an incident that I couldn't seem to escape from. As I may have lost my good conduct which was the last thing I ever wanted.

After having a few dances with a local girl, I asked if she would accompany me to the cinema the following evening in Northampton and she accepted. It was on the condition that I would be back at Quebec Barracks by 10pm. That was the curfew time. On seeing the film, we waited at a bus stop for the 9pm bus to arrive but unfortunately it never appeared. So we had to wait another hour for the 10pm bus, which did arrive promptly. We had no alternative than to wait, as I was in no position to order a taxi, as what money I did have had been spent that evening at the pictures. Finally, the 10pm bus did arrive and by this time I knew I'd be in trouble regardless of whatever time I managed to arrive back at Quebec Barracks. I was grateful that the 10pm bus had arrived otherwise I could have been away from the barracks for many more hours. The girl lived in the village of Wootton, only a mile from the barracks. When we departed from the bus, it just happened to be a very dark and a cold winter's evening and hardly safe for a young girl to walk home on her own. I quickly realised it was my responsibility to escort the girl home, irrespective of the consequences of what time I would arrive back at Quebec Barracks.

On the long walk I took to reach the barracks, I had much to think about and I knew that I would be in serious trouble. In the guardroom, two of the guards did not extend any sympathy towards me concerning the 9pm bus, which hadn't arrived at its scheduled time in Northampton. Now, I know if I had been late by a couple of minutes it may have been OK but to be late by over two hours was just not acceptable. It didn't seem to matter whatever excuse I came up with the two guards were not at all interested. They seemed quite aggressive in their attitude towards me and I feared I might possibly be spending the night in the cells. They promptly informed me, that in view of the seriousness of the situation I'd be put on a charge which meant appearing in front of the Commanding Officer of Quebec Barracks, who would then decide what punishment I should have.

A week later, I was being marched in double quick time into the Commanding Officer's office and saluted Colonel Barber. I felt like saying my prayers as I waited for the punishment that I was likely to receive as he read the report about my lateness. I had already been told that the C.O. could be rather severe in his sentence of any wrong doings on my part, and I pleaded guilty. I did fear the worst, as I had no alternative to admit to being late by over two and a half hours, but I did mention the 9pm bus not turning up, again no one was listening. With the Easter break being the following weekend, I also feared I'd be doing menial jobs at the barracks all over the Easter weekend. This would mean not seeing my family over that time. On passing his judgement on me Colonel Barber did show some compassion and mentioned it wasn't entirely my fault for being late. So, instead of the four days of jankers expected I received two days. I felt the C.O. understood the position I'd found myself in. I felt he had been fair to me and I thought I'd got off lightly.

"My National Service is part of my training for freeing my soul from the bondage of the flesh."

Mahatma Gandhi.

8

Jankers

The unusual name of Jankers is not listed in the English Dictionary but I do believe it has a history going back to the First World War. The origins may have been given after a British soldier with the surname Jankers, who had done something wrong. He would have been put on a charge and if found guilty the punishment would be so many days of doing menial jobs – Jankers.

I was still slightly annoyed by the outcome of my offence, as I think I had a genuine excuse, but I was to learn very quickly that in the British Army, excuses mean nothing at all. Only the real facts mattered and the overwhelming fact was that I was over two hours late on reporting back to Quebec Barracks guardroom, which I couldn't dispute. In the British Army one learns fast and excuses whatever the cause are simply never enough.

My two days of jankers was to start on Good Friday morning at 6am and finish on the Saturday evening. As I wasn't going anywhere I must have looked a rather dejected figure when I wished Les and other friends in the barrack room much enjoyment on their Easter weekend. I can recall what a lonesome existence it all was: where I missed all the barrack room chatter, (which always went on well into the evening) where I found that being on my own I was not just one person in my barrack room but the only one in the whole of a large building. Fortunately, there were still a few soldiers on the camp, otherwise it looked as though everyone had deserted a sinking ship. I'm also sure that when Sergeant Davis first heard I had been put on jankers over Easter, he would show no sympathy and he would have laughed his socks off.

On Good Friday morning I was up at the usual time of 6am. I had to report to the cookhouse where I was ordered to help serve the breakfast for the few soldiers who remained at Quebec Barracks. Then, mopping out the cookhouse and the kitchen was the top priority of my work and the majority of my time was spent peeling potatoes, involving hundreds of spuds. One of the worst jobs I was required to do was to clean several toilets. I found this degrading and it had the most revolting smell. I began to think I was nothing but a common criminal at times. This was, after all, a punishment that I never wanted to experience again. Then it was back to peeling spuds. For those two days it became one of the most boring jobs going. Even so I still preferred it to swilling out stinking toilets. The only thing that kept me civilised was the thought that I would soon be going home. At that time I believed I hated the army and the fear was, once home I wouldn't want to return to Quebec Barracks. Perish the thought!

Jankers over. I'm not sure whether I caught a bus or a train back to Peterborough, that Sunday morning. As I strode into our home in Stanground with a huge smile on my face it felt so very good to be home with all the familiar surroundings that I'd known for years. This included my parents and my three brothers who had equally waited for me to give an update of my experiences so far in the army.

To be with my parents again was definitely a big bonus as far as I was concerned and they must have worried when I was late to arrive home for the Easter weekend. My father, without being judgemental, said to me,

"As regards the jankers, learn from it boy and make sure it never happens again."

But my Mother being more protective of me, remarked that,

"It wasn't your fault that the bus never turned up that night."

Being home for just a few hours with my family made me realise how much my family meant to me. If I'd let them down I could only apologise but it was marvellous just to see them all. Being home acted as a sort of pick me up. I most definitely felt better on that brief visit, so much so, that when I returned to Quebec Barracks I was full of optimism that my life in the army could only get better.

*"Everybody can be great ...
because anybody can serve."*

Martin Luther King Jr.

9

The Essex Regiment

Towards the end of basic training at Quebec Barracks and with the Passing Out Parade approaching fast, we were given the devastating news that the recruits in B Company would not be joining the 2nd Battalion of the Northamptonshire Regiment in Hong Kong, as the regiment would soon be returning home to England. To say I was disappointed is a gross understatement as I was really looking forward to seeing that part of the world just to have my hopes dashed. Unless the Regiment was sent somewhere else abroad I'd be spending all my National Service in Great Britain, which filled me with much despair.

Another reason I didn't want to serve my National Service in Great Britain was that I didn't want to arrive home every weekend. Making that statement is by no means a reflection on my parents. I had the very best of parents imaginable, I just didn't want to be applying for weekend leave all the time as I hadn't any commitments whatsoever to entice me home. I couldn't see the point of it all. If I were to see Hong

Kong it would help me to see how much the British Army had played its part in the security of the place, as there was a real possibility that China may cross over the border and invade Hong Kong. (Many years later China did cross over the border without a shot being fired.) The disappointment didn't last long, about a week actually, when the quite unbelievable happened! We were informed that we would be going to Hong Kong after all, by being transferred to the 2nd Battalion of the Essex Regiment, who were already serving in Hong Kong.

Evidently, the transfer of recruits from one regiment to another is a regular practice and this time it was recruits from B Company who would be going. The reason given was the Essex Regiment was understaffed at that particular time in Hong Kong. There were some recruits who may have regretted leaving the Northamptonshire Regiment, as a good 90% of the recruits were born in the county and had close family links to Northamptonshire, but they had to accept what was happening and swallow their pride. This was also a regret for me as I was leaving the regiment in which my father and uncle had served during the First World War.

Another possible worry was; would the lads from the Essex Regiment extend a warm welcome to the lads of the Northamptonshire Regiment who were joining them? They might have resented us. There can often be some indignation when soldiers are transferred in this way but it remained to be seen what the consequences might be. I was once again thrilled beyond words that Hong Kong beckoned and I couldn't wait, having worked constantly hard, every day, for nearly seven weeks on the Square.

I thought it had become very obvious that there had been a remarkable transformation in the recruits drill work. Sometimes, I actually thought we were all enjoying the square bashing as the squad responded accordingly and precisely in formation to any order that was being shouted out; with the marching being impeccably done, with everyone in step. It must have been an absolute joy to see rifles being used correctly in 'slope arms', 'present arms' and 'order arms' in response to the orders given.

I'm sure we might have thought that everything to do with the squad was a mere formality by just turning up and giving a good performance on the actual day. How wrong could we be? Sergeant Davis went ballistic in his criticism of us by saying that we had not reached the required standard and that we had become complacent and to think otherwise was a complete travesty. What he said of us was completely true and was a wakeup call. He finished by informing us that we would now work twice as hard as before. We then heard that Sergeant Davis would be retiring from the army after the Passing Out Parade, so obviously he wanted to go out on a high. We decided that we must give the best performance we were capable of giving, as it would be a special day for him, but he continued to give me a hard time. My friend Les noticed this and warned me,

"Sergeant Davis has got it in for you, so watch out!"

Les was right, so I became more aware of Sergeant Davis' behaviour and how he tried to belittle me in front of other soldiers. Any respect I had for him receded quickly, but later he came to feel more positive towards me, much to my eternal satisfaction.

"I am the astronaut of boxing.
Joe Louis and Dempsey were just jet pilots.
I'm in a world of my own."

Muhammad Ali.

10

Boxing Days

No, it wasn't the day after Christmas, but real live boxing days. During all the hours in training spent (mostly on the square) that a boxing tournament had been arranged for the entertainment of all the soldiers of Quebec Barracks. All that was required was anyone who was interested to put their names forward.

Although, I hadn't put on any boxing gloves for about three years, I still felt fit enough to allow myself to volunteer in the hope I could still make a contribution and hopefully stage a good fight. I know my friend Les thought I was absolutely mad to volunteer for such a tournament, but I had been involved in boxing right from a young age.

At the age of twelve I boxed in the local garden fête, at Stanground where I lived, and also when I attended Stamford School where I made it into the school boxing team. At fifteen, I was training with the Peterborough Boxing Club. So I was hardly a novice to the boxing game.

My brother Michael, who was five years older than me, was probably the reason I became interested in boxing - he boxed and could look after himself. What didn't help Michael was that he was a poor scholar at school and was often taken advantage of by classmates. When returning home from school he might have a black eye or some other deformity. Once when the bridge fair was on in the city, he was persuaded by friends that if he would fight a professional boxer in the boxing ring and somehow managed to stay on his feet he would win five pounds, which he did but he received a terrible beating but what guts he had.

It was in the gym at Quebec Barracks that the Gym Sergeant would assess who one's opponent would be. Evidently, Sergeant Davis was a boxing enthusiast and it was then that I learned that my opponent was a real tough looking character. I immediately became suspicious that Sergeant Davis was the instigator of such a fight probably thinking that I couldn't possibly win and was likely to get a real beating at the same time. If that was the case, I had to prove him wrong. My determination was increased significantly, which was just the spur I needed to win the fight.

All the boxing bouts that day meant that there were eight such bouts in all, each having three rounds. Over many years, these boxing bouts created lots of interest and the gym was packed to the rafters. All the excitement was very evident indeed for such an occasion. I then learned that my fight was the last bout of the afternoon.

Unfortunately, I had a long time to wait which played havoc with my nervous system. All negative thoughts started to appear and I became increasingly anxious. I began to question myself why I had entered into such a competition, as I hadn't boxed for a number of years? Perhaps Les was right when he thought I was mad but I also knew that he would be rooting for me. Was I nervous? You bet I was, because I knew absolutely nothing about my opponent.

When it was my turn to enter the boxing ring and on seeing my opponent's muscular body, I wasn't filled with confidence one little bit. However, I was receiving massive support from new-found friends in the barrack room who gave me the feeling I couldn't let them down and because of their support I became fired up once more. I won on points as I was fast around the ring and at the age of nineteen I carried no weight at all, being very much a fly-weight boxer. By moving quickly, I managed to escape many of my opponent's hammer blows whereas if he had caught me I could have been knocked out.

I realized I had lost none of my enthusiasm for boxing, which I had gained while growing up in Stanground. Sergeant Davis had a front row seat and if he expected me to lose, to what he thought was a superior opponent; he must have felt very disappointed that I had won. I had proved to him that I was no pushover. I need not have worried as from that day onwards in his eyes I could do no wrong and his attitude to me changed completely (shame on him that I had to prove myself in the boxing ring in the first place). By winning that boxing bout my eagerness for boxing returned. The boxing tournament had been a big success and there would be another and I looked forward to when I would box again.

"The soldier is the Army.
No army is better than its soldiers.
The Soldier is also a citizen.
In fact, the highest obligation and privilege of
citizenship is that of bearing arms for one's
country."

George S. Patton Jr.

11

A Few Extras

Night-time Exercises

We were involved in a military night time manoeuvre exercise. We blacked our faces on a very dark, wet and cold winter's night in the hope that the 'enemy' wouldn't see us. Evidently, the 'enemy' had also blacked their faces so we didn't see them either. This took place deep in the Northamptonshire countryside and, all things considered, seemed to me a complete waste of time.

On reflection many years later it fills me with much amusement, how on earth can two different lots of soldiers with black faces find each other on the blackest of winter nights imaginable. Even now I can't stop laughing about it.

Meals

The meals in the cookhouse were reasonable but there was never enough food on our plates to satisfy growing teenage boys, who all had big appetites. No wonder we would occasionally visit the NAAFI as we were often hungry. Any food we bought from the NAAFI had to be paid for out of our own pocket, no wonder we were always skint! Our wages as a National Service soldier were deplorable, although if we had signed on for another year, making it three years in all, we would receive a small increase in pay, which still wasn't enough in order to have a decent life.

When on home leave, in the early days, at Quebec Barracks my mother would fill my dinner plate and say, *"I've got to feed you well as the Army doesn't seem to bother."*

Sports

As a keen footballer, I really missed not playing, apart from a kick about, although I did play regular football after the Passing Out Parade. There were facilities at the barracks involving snooker and table tennis but we just didn't have the time or inclination to play.

Cricket was my favourite sport, but I had been told it was only played by the officers. I knew I would miss the game very much indeed. But I knew that in Hong Kong lots of cricket is played there so hopefully, I might get a game but at this stage I lived in hope. To be honest – it never happened.

Part of our training was to visit the gym every week. I've always enjoyed physical exercise and the gym, of course, was useful for when I took up boxing again. I tried to get back in prime condition for the next two boxing bouts I had at Quebec Barracks. I would have liked to have made progress in this sport but I simply wasn't good enough.

Lectures

We were always attending lectures, which were usually about the army. However, there was one particular lecture given emphatically by Lieutenant Evans-Evans. His lecture highlighted prostitution and venereal disease (VD) in Hong Kong, and we were warned to stay away from the women who carried this disease.

More Injections

When we knew we were going to Hong Kong, we had numerous injections to make us immune to specific diseases. (Eventually I began to feel like a pin cushion.) Some soldiers really did have a fear of injections, often passing out or they might feel unwell for a day or so, but fortunately it never affected me.

23115506 Private B W Holdich. Passing Out Parade.
1st Battalion of the Northamptonshire Regiment.
Taken at Quebec Barracks.

12

The Passing Out Parade

The proposed time of the Passing Out Parade escapes me, it could have been the end of April 1955. This was a red letter day when on a Saturday all the recruits of Quebec Barracks would at last be qualified as soldiers, provided everything went well once we were on the drill square that afternoon. Looking back, we'd had nine weeks of square bashing, been pushed to the limits by Sergeant Davis and Corporal Waller. I think Corporal Waller was a real decent type of individual who may have thought that Sergeant Davis was pushing us too hard but I never heard him utter one word against the Sergeant.

Lieutenant Evans-Evans was leading us that day and we waited at the side of the square where Sergeant Davis and Corporal Waller were giving us last minute instructions. In view of the importance of the occasion, the Regimental Sergeant Major was in charge as usual. I do not remember his name but I do remember the harshness of his voice (he certainly didn't wish for us to fall asleep). This was the day of reckoning when hopefully all the recruits would feel much fulfilment of a job well done.

Our uniforms had been ironed several times over with the creases on the trouser legs being so sharp one could cut oneself. If looks and general smartness was anything to go by we had absolutely nothing to fear. Dazzling in the sun that day (on every beret), was the regimental badge of the Northamptonshire Regiment. We would probably be wearing it for the very last time before all the squad on the square were transferred to the Essex Regiment. As regards to one's boots, it goes without saying that one could see one's face on looking down at the toe caps.

Now the whole squad was set for a great send off and the pressure building up was immense having literally rehearsed the parade drill hundreds of times. Our confidence was sky high. Surely though we couldn't get it wrong, could we?

The order to come to attention was given by the Regimental Sergeant Major. At that precise moment the squad of one hundred heavy boots clattered on the concrete square with split second timing in formation. We were given the order to 'slope arms' with our rifles finishing up on our left shoulder, the left hand holding the butt of the rifle, which was also done in synchronized formation.

The next order to be given was, *"By the Left, Quick March"*, and at that command the Northamptonshire Regimental Band proceeded to play. The squad began marching with the right arms moving shoulder high and in step with the military music being played. I'm sure it gave us all an inevitable lift, which made that afternoon even more imposing.

By this time, the squad was approaching Colonel Barber who was standing on a pedestal in front of a large gathering of people who had come to watch the parade. As the squad marched by the Colonel, we were ordered to give him 'eyes right', this means a slight turn of the head, and the Colonel saluted in return. As I turned my head to the right, I saw all the people who had come to watch the occasion. I spotted my mother wandering about and looking lost, apparently she was searching for my father. She was at that time only a few feet from Colonel Barber and she may have thought to herself, 'why are all the soldiers looking at me?' My mother would have had no idea that we were giving an 'eyes right' to the Colonel and definitely not to her, it's a wonder my dear mother didn't start waving back in return. I have to say my mother could be very naïve at times, God bless her.

I'm testing my memories as to the exact procedures of that day but I'm fairly sure we marched halfway round the square and the squad finished directly in front of Colonel Barber. The band was playing the National Anthem and we presented arms with our rifles and the Colonel saluted once more. Next, Colonel Barber left the pedestal to inspect the dress (a soldier's dress on formal parade was his best uniform). When the Colonel inspected me I'm not sure that he recognised me, but what I do know is, if my dress had been untidy or even slovenly I'd be back peeling the spuds before one could say, 'jankers'.

After the inspection we marched off the square to thunderous applause. We had excelled ourselves with a brilliant performance, we couldn't possibly have done it better, with spilt second timing in formation. I was told it was a joy to behold. Sergeant Davis who worked so hard with us was to be congratulated.

He was over the moon and couldn't stop smiling. If he was leaving the army he hadn't chosen a better time. I know at times I found him unpredictable in his attitude towards me but I bore him no animosity whatsoever. Perhaps, the feelings between us were difficult at the start but ultimately we finished as friends (which is better than enemies). Anyway, life is too short to fall out with anyone.

The whole event took just over one hour and the support we received was incredible. Amongst the crowds were; many mums and dads, brothers and sisters, many girlfriends, other relatives and friends who helped to create a really wonderful atmosphere. Everyone, including my parents, had been delighted in what they witnessed.

Once the parade was over, we were allowed to take our guests over the whole area of Quebec Barracks. I'm sure my father, being an ex-soldier, was impressed with what he saw. We visited the gymnasium, the NAAFI, the guardroom and the cookhouse, where for much of my two days of jankers, I had been peeling spuds in the kitchen. As we stood in the kitchen, I informed my mother to never ask me to peel the potatoes when I'm home, I was sick of the sight of them, but I had learned an important lesson concerning Jankers, never again!

Finally, I took my parents to the barrack room that had been my home for nine weeks where I found the place full of excitement about the day. The camaraderie was simply astonishing, everyone was laughing and joking with each other. This was nothing like the situation just a few short weeks before, when we were strangers looking at our neighbours either side of us with some suspicion, and indeed mistrust, as to whom that person really was. Now, these strangers had become good friends.

All of the recruits were now fully-fledged soldiers, having served their time most satisfactorily in their nine weeks training. The day resulted in many handshakes all round. My parents met Les and his parents. My mother thanked Les for looking after me. Les quickly responded to that compliment by saying, *"You have got that the wrong way round, Mrs Holdich, because it was Brian who looked after me!"* I then introduced my parents to Lieutenant Evans-Evans and Sergeant Davis who were both mixing generally with everyone in the barrack room. My father thanked both of them saying,

"Thank you for making a man of my son."

His words really surprised me but deep down I knew my father was absolutely right.

Before the army discipline straightened me out, I rebelled too much at home and was considered a tearaway, often causing my parents considerable worry with reckless behaviour. I'm sure my dad, noticed the change after my service and he was such a good man I did not want to let him down ever again. I therefore tried to live up to his high expectations and was surprised by what he said about me. I knew he was proud of me, and I couldn't have asked for more.

"I learned that courage was not the absence of fear, but the triumph over it. The brave man is not he who does not feel afraid, but he who conquers that fear."

Nelson Mandela.

13

Embarkation Leave

After the triumphant success of the Passing Out Parade we were given one week's leave. I did hope it wouldn't be too long before we set sail for Hong Kong and the Far East, but actually we didn't leave Quebec Barracks for another three months. Life at the barracks proceeded much as before with plenty of square bashing and physical exercise to keep us in good shape.

Now we were soldiers, we had a new schedule of guard duties, which meant at night time we were patrolling the whole of the camp area in pairs. We had live ammunition in our rifles in case we saw people trespassing or acting in a suspicious manner. Fortunately, not a shot was fired.

I was hoping that while at the barracks I would make it into the Battalion football team, but it was summertime and in those days, no football was played during the summer months. I would occasionally play cricket when I was home (for Peterborough Town Cricket Club) but I was not playing regularly enough to compete for a place in the First Team, being unable to get home every weekend.

We attended even more lectures about Hong Kong and the situation concerning China's troops crossing over the border to invade Hong Kong. Any soldier of a nervous disposition it would find it very worrying and indeed frightening. However, soldiers are only human like the rest of us and when put to the test some are braver than others.

While waiting for a ship to take us to Hong Kong it was decided to stage another boxing tournament. In this competition I won against my opponent, on points but I didn't get the same satisfaction of this win. It looked as if my opponent had never been in a boxing ring before unlike my previous fight, in which my opponent had been as tough as old nails and would never throw in the towel. The most worrying aspect of boxing in the army was that one would know absolutely nothing about one's opponent. They might be someone of huge potential who would climb all the way up the ladder. Looking at the intake of new recruits arriving at Quebec Barracks, who was going to dispute the fact that a future 'Boxing Champion' might be among them.

At last, after what seemed like an eternity, we knew when we would be leaving for Hong Kong (around the beginning of August 1955). This time, for sure, we would be sailing from Southampton. I had really looked forward to this phase of my life as a great adventure and thought how fortunate I was in comparison to other servicemen who hadn't been given such an opportunity.

We were presented with ten days embarkation leave and during this time I seemed to be saying goodbye to everyone that knew me. Notably, many aunts and uncles; other relatives, such as distant cousins; and also to ex-work colleagues at the Peterborough Power Station and those friends from the sports clubs I belonged to. My mother had insisted on this, otherwise people would think how rude I was.

I shall always remember the stern warning one aunt in particular said to me,

"When young boys leave home and go abroad the temptations are very strong. You are to behave yourself in Hong Kong and not bring disgrace to the family name, which you would regret for the rest of your life." Wise words that I never forgot.

Unfortunately though, that piece of advice placed a burden on me that nearly put the damper on nearly everything I was to become involved with. I do believe my aunt meant well and I suppose being only nineteen years of age I may have been vulnerable and inexperienced to the dangers of the world and their attractions. Surely, there was no harm in me looking at a most attractive Chinese girl who was walking towards me was there? I told my father what his sister had said to me and he smiled saying, *"Just behave yourself that's all I ask."*

My mother at the time of my departure was naturally upset like any mother would be, as I would be away for well over a year. I had only one mother and I loved her dearly, but she knew I wanted to see the world, which was going to be an education in itself, if only to see how the other half of the world lived. The experience that I was about to undertake would be invaluable on my personal journey to manhood. Although I was still a teenager, I felt that I had a lot to learn.

I said goodbye to my parents and brothers and then I was on my way, catching the train back to Northampton. Here I was reunited with the same two soldiers I had met when the three of us were travelling to Quebec Barracks to begin our National Service. The journey I was about to undertake, had been harboured in my mind for some time and I was still in a state of high excitement of what was about to happen. I only hoped it would live up to all the expectations I had placed before myself otherwise I would be terribly disappointed.

Our Regiment left Quebec Barracks early the following morning by coach, which took about six hours to reach Southampton. We made for the dock area and it became apparent that literally hundreds of other soldiers from various different regiments throughout Great Britain were all lined up also waiting to board the troopship H.M. Dilwara. I did wonder at that time, how on earth this troopship would be able to take all these soldiers and it looked to me that we would be overloaded. In front of us was a large squad of soldiers who belonged to the 2nd Battalion of the Essex Regiment. The very same regiment we would be in, and in conversation they wanted to know where we had come from. On realising we were now in the same regiment but not Essex boys by birth, I felt there was some indignation against us. In contrast, these Essex soldiers were from the inner city, London boys, who originated from Dagenham, Barking and Canning Town. They may have felt that we were intruders by joining their regiment, but we certainly couldn't help it, having had no choice as to where we were transferred to the Essex Regiment or any other regiment for that matter.

14

The Troopship H.M. Dilwara

It seemed like many hours of waiting before we could board the Dilwara. We had to find the appropriate troop deck, which would be our sleeping quarters for the next few weeks. The decks were overcrowded with bodies, kit bags and other luggage, which was scattered all over the place. I dumped my kit bag on my bunk bed and Les and I made for the top deck of the ship to have our last look at the old country.

We slowly drifted away from everything we loved about England, which would always be our home wherever we might be sent. We must have stayed on the top deck of the Dilwara troopship for nearly an hour and I can still remember that day most significantly as we set sail for the Far East with approximately five hundred other British servicemen on board. I was sure there were several other troop decks to accommodate every one of them.

Les and I returned to our troop deck to find it was overflowing with many soldiers trying to find a bunk bed to sleep on. Les, being unable to find a bunk bed near me settled for one elsewhere. I quickly discovered I was surrounded by those homegrown Essex boys who this time were most friendly and helpful. They went out of their way to welcome me into the Essex Regiment and I realised that I had misjudged them earlier that day. All the beds on the troop deck were bunk beds, which were constructed with one bunk bed situated on the top of another bunk bed, making it three bunk beds in all.

My bunk bed was at the bottom of the other two beds. This meant that if the occupiers above me turned over in their sleep, the springs on the beds would make a hell of a noise. I had the constant fear that the two beds above me would come crashing down. All these bunk beds were designed to create more space, in order that the troop decks could carry even more soldiers. The gangways were also quite narrow.

What didn't help that day was someone had been trying to open my kit bag, obviously there was a thief about. We had already been warned that it was our responsibility to make sure that our kit bags were well looked after otherwise we would have to pay for the cost of anything stolen.

The Troopship H.M. Dilwara

My brief history of the troopship H.M. Dilwara is as follows; she was built in Glasgow and was launched on the 17th October 1935. She was the first British troopship built since 1876.

In 1939, when war broke out, she was first used as a troopship from South Africa to Egypt, and then in 1942 she was present at the Madagascar Landings. In 1943, she took part in the Sicilian Campaign and then in 1945 she was involved in the liberation of Burma.

Later in 1945, she was mined off Rangoon with major damages. She was the HQ ship during the surrender of operations in Singapore.

After the Second World War most of her employment was between the Far East and Great Britain including service in the Korean War. In 1953, she was at the Coronation Review at Spithead, and in 1956 she was involved in the Suez Crisis. Later in 1960, her trooping contract was finally terminated and at the end of that year the Dilwara was sold to China. However, in 1962 she re-emerged to begin off-season cruising from Australia and New Zealand, then finally in November 1971 she was sold again and broken up in Taiwan. The Dilwara along with other troopships had a great history particularly in wartime.

The Troopship H.M. Dilwara.

*"To give real service you must add
something which cannot be bought
or measured with money,
and that is sincerity and integrity."*

Douglas Adams.

15

The Blue Mediterranean

I never expected a good night's sleep that first night on a troop deck in the English Channel and sure enough, I didn't receive one. During the night, I can recall some instances of excessive noise by fellow passengers, which were startling and disturbed my sleep. I was also aware of the ship's engines, which wasn't all that quiet at times but there was nothing unduly to worry about. Yet, once out of my bunk bed early the next morning I came to the conclusion that, as the Dilwara approached the Atlantic Ocean, those stormy seas were ahead of us. This was where we experienced a real rough and rocky ride. After a couple of days it certainly wasn't any better in the Bay of Biscay, when during this period I did see a few soldiers being violently sick. Fortunately, it never happened to me so I was really lucky in that respect, but soon we would be out of such disrupted waters and we hoped to see some sunshine.

Our first sight of land was the appearance of the Rock of Gibraltar, standing out like a sore thumb, and considering it is such a famous landmark, it was not a pretty sight. It would have been ideal if we could have had a day's shore leave in Gibraltar being that it was under British Rule. This still exists today, as one of the last of Britain's colonies still under the rule of the British Empire. At their last referendum, Gibraltarians voted overwhelmingly to remain ruled by Great Britain (much to the annoyance of Spain). It would have been so interesting to have seen Gibraltar, which I believe was the spitting image of the old country.

It brought back memories; as a young school boy all those years ago, of one lady school teacher in particular. In religious studies one day I thought she went overboard in describing the wonders of the Mediterranean Sea. She informed the class how blue the waters were and how very clean and so clear that one could nearly see the bottom of this incredible looking sea. So on leaving Gibraltar, it was as if a door was opened up to the most placid and perfect world imaginable, creating for us the most beautiful of settings. I began to realise that my school teacher was right in her description of the Mediterranean Sea and yes the sea was so blue that one really could see a long way down.

It was over sixty years ago when I first saw the Mediterranean Sea and it was a really extraordinary sight to see. Nowadays, it is likely that all seas and rivers across the whole world today are far more polluted far more than ever. It is quite possible I really did see the Mediterranean Sea at its best.

The only other place which affected me in the same way, was the Taj Mahal in India which I visited in 1991. This also gave me wonderful memories for being, simply magnificent. The Taj Mahal's splendour was a contrast to the deplorable squalor of the big cities of New Dehli and Calcutta where I was constantly reminded of the day I visited Colombo in Ceylon.

"The miracle is not that we do this work,
but that we are happy to do it."

Mother Teresa

16

We're Busy Doin' Nothing

"We're busy doin' nothing,
Working the whole day through,
Tryin' to find lots of things not to do
We're busy goin' nowhere
Isn't it just a crime
We'd like to be unhappy, but
We never do have the time."

The above words were sung by a trio, namely Bing Crosby, Cedrick Hardwick and William Bendix, who starred in the musical comedy, 'A Yank in King Arthur's Court'. I would have been about fifteen years of age when I first saw the film. For weeks afterwards I'd be forever singing this hit song from the film. Now, on the troopship Dilwara, I could see a similarity to the film as for much of the time many servicemen had a busy time doing nothing.

We were laid out on a troop deck under the glorious sunshine in the Mediterranean Sea, where I suppose for some it could have been boring, but for Les and I, it felt as though we were on holiday having won a lottery and not being in the army.

As in the song, *'We're Busy Doin' Nothing'* it continued to remind me that doing nothing was not hard to do. So, what did the soldiers do apart from lying in the sun all day? Well, there was a certain amount of work to be done but usually all work would be completed by twelve, noon. After an early breakfast at 7am, all the soldiers would have to attend the Muster Parade where every soldier was counted in by regiment. At the same time there would be a fire drill, which was really important as many a ship over the years had caught fire. Every soldier would know what was expected of him in the event of fire. Rather surprisingly and very pleasingly, the army dress seemed to have been abandoned. We would be going through very hot weather with only shorts and a shirt needed. We still had to wash, shower and shave and generally keep clean for our own personal satisfaction irrespective of being in the army or not.

We all shared in various different jobs. We had been allocated one of the worst. The daily cleaning out of our troop deck where the smell was intolerable though this was understandable in view of the number of soldiers sleeping there. Otherwise, we kept fit with regular PE sessions or a walk around the ship—anything to keep the joints moving!

After a week at sea, it became unmistakeable that a thief (or thieves) were about and they had broken into my kit bag and stolen some clothing. I was quite livid about this, having been told previously that anything lost on the ship would have to be paid for, by me, once the regiment reached Hong Kong. This was very worrying. I have mentioned that I was surrounded by Essex boys in the troop deck, not the lads who had been transferred with me from the Northamptonshire Regiment. In the short time I had known these lads I found that I got along with them really well. However, there were four that slept opposite my own bunk bed of whom I'd become suspicious. I hadn't got the necessary proof that they had been in my kit bag and because of that situation I couldn't accuse anyone. So, it meant being my usual self and talking normally to everyone as if nothing had happened. I realised this was not a position I favoured but I had no history with these Essex lads (were they trustworthy or not?)

I did casually mention the plight I was in to a corporal who quickly informed me that there was a lot of stealing going on. I also mentioned to Les who was some distance from me on the troop deck and he had heard the same. I definitely had my suspicions but felt my hands were tied behind my back and I couldn't trust anyone. *"What was I to do?"* I kept asking myself. Then I found the culprit, or one of them. I had returned early one afternoon to my troop deck and there underneath my bunk bed was one of the four of whom I was suspicious. On seeing me, he quickly got up and said, stuttering, *"Sorry mate, I've just dropped something and it rolled under your bed."* He was retrieving it, or so he said, but I didn't believe him. I sensed he was lying as the other three were grinning. Now sometimes I am able to get worked up if needed and this was one such situation. However, I told myself to refrain and do nothing as the time wasn't right. (The time came soon enough in all places - the boxing ring!)

The long voyage by the ship in the Mediterranean Sea from Gibraltar to Port Said in Egypt, meant that we had travelled over two thousand miles, and the Dilwara put down its anchor half a mile from the Port. Most of the soldiers, including myself, were on the top deck of the Dilwara taking in what we could see of Port Said. Once again we hadn't been given any shore leave, and were confined to the ship. It would have been really nice once more to walk as normal on the ground rather than experiencing the constant roll of the ship, no matter how gentle the sea may have been.

When the Dilwara dropped its anchor it was a message for all the Dumboats, and there were dozens of them, to make for the troopship. This was an opportunity for these poor peasant people to come alongside our ship and try to sell whatever it was they were selling, usually fruit or clothes. The selling of goods was achieved by: first agreeing a price; then lowering a basket from the ship; and the goods being placed in the basket and hauled back up to the buyer and then the agreed price of the money put into the basket and lowered to the seller below.

The Dilwara must have left Port Said late that evening as it was daylight when I awoke the following morning and we found ourselves in the Suez Canal. To see dry land either side of us was a really comforting sight. I found the Canal was not all that wide for all those heavy loaded ships, which are used most frequently. I always thought it was Great Britain who built the Suez Canal, which was a hundred miles long, linking the Mediterranean Sea to the Red Sea and had proved to be an outstanding success. However, it was actually a Frenchman who was given the contract to build the Suez Canal in 1854. Previously, Egypt had been ruled by Great Britain for seventy-five years and the relationship between the two countries was often strained. The building of the Canal meant that the long journey around the Cape of South Africa was shortened by thousands of miles. This meant that ships could deliver their cargo many weeks earlier than before, much to the satisfaction of countries worldwide.

"We ourselves feel that what we are doing
is just a drop in the ocean.
But the ocean would be less
because of that missing drop."

Mother Teresa.

17

The Red Sea

Our troopship Dilwara spent a few hours in the
Suez Canal. We were to see a few pyramids and
the odd camel, where the only excitement I can recall
was to see a few youngsters running and waving in
harmony along the banks of the Canal, in their efforts
to keep up with us. However, as time progressed by,
I was gradually coming to the conclusion that being
on a ship in the Suez Canal could be very tedious
indeed, as the Canal never had any twists or turns.
It was straight as an arrow with the landscape either
side of the Canal being nothing more than sand.

At this time, the heat was really sweltering with
not one flicker of wind to be felt anywhere as we
approached the Red Sea. In the whole of my life,
neither before nor since that time, have I experienced
such a scorching heat or temperatures as high. Every
single soldier on that ship was sweating (buckets
full) and certainly no-one was sunbathing. If they
had tried to, they would have had a serious attack
of sunstroke and died. Yes, that blistering sun was
sheer murder!

During the night time, when the Dilwara was travelling through the Red Sea, it was so hot in the troop's decks that many soldiers found it impossible to sleep because of such over-crowdedness. It was probably the most unhealthiest and unfortunate place I've ever tried to go to sleep in. The high temperatures meant many soldiers were talking throughout the night, keeping those who could sleep awake. Everyone continued to sweat profusely. These old style troop decks were appalling places, particularly during hot weather.

After a long and 'leisurely' ship cruise, the Dilwara made for the Gulf of Aden in South Yemen. This is often regarded as the poorest of the Arab States in the Middle East. Along with its neighbour, Yemen, it was ruled by the British until 1967 when it became a Marxist, One Party State and the British Forces had left the country. Britain for many years afterwards recognised the importance of the Suez Canal remaining open and in particular, the value of the capital, Aden, as a port controlling the southern entrance to the Red Sea.

South Yemen is a country of extremely high temperatures with a range from 32°C (90°F) to 38°C (100°F) in summertime. I know all the lads on the troop deck were really looking forward to the delights of what Aden could offer us as we had all been offered shore leave at last. We couldn't wait to leave the Dilwara and to get our legs operating correctly again. There really was genuine excitement as to what sort of day it would be. However, it was without question, a major disappointment as none of us could get to Aden before twelve, noon, after which everywhere was closed. We discovered that

66

on the day we were given for visiting Aden was half day closing. A lot of the lads were grumbling and cursed this fact. (How could it possibly be a half day closing?) We couldn't find one shop open and Aden looked like a ghost town, being virtually empty. The only consolation was, we all managed a good walk and we were grateful for that.

The next day, after the dissatisfaction of not seeing Aden at its best, the Dilwara proceeded to make its way out of the Gulf of Aden and make for the Arabian Sea. Another long ship ride of nearly two thousand miles to Ceylon, which gave us many hours of sunbathing. For the life of me, I cannot remember a swimming pool on the Dilwara but I do recall the many cold showers taken in order to cool down. So what entertainment was there for the troops aboard the Dilwara?

There were countless films available in the evening to watch. Les and I would usually like a pint of beer in the evenings and in those days we were both smokers. We didn't have much money left to join other pursuits like cards or dominoes, and Les would spend hours writing to his girlfriend. As regards to receiving letters from home, wherever the ship stopped there was always hordes of mail for Les but much less for me. So, to receive my mother's weekly letter was absolutely paramount to me. I myself, could hardly be called an avid letter writer in those days but I wrote to my parents once a week and that was all my mother asked of me.

Boxing, it appeared, was the ideal sport to keep all the troops on the Dilwara well entertained, so a boxing tournament had been arranged. As I'd won my two previous fights, I again volunteered. I had kept in good shape with many regular PE sessions. While there was still some thieving going on once it was known that I was a boxer and would be taking part in a boxing tournament I seemed to get more respect. I came to the conclusion that because of this those homegrown Essex boys became friendlier. I appreciated this, but as my bunk bed happened to be well away from my good friends in the former Northamptonshire Regiment, I was not only pleased but quite relieved that most of the thieving had stopped. At that time, having been personally stolen from, it felt that I was in a den of thieves. It wasn't just one regiment who were implicated in the theft of my army clothes, but about four other regiments who were also represented on our troop deck. This created an awful lot of suspicion as to whom one could trust and to whom one could not.

The boxing ring for the competition day had been placed on the top deck, on the Port side of the ship. There were eight boxing bouts each of three rounds. There were over two hundred spectators and they would have sat on the funnels in order to be there. The atmosphere was terrific. Eventually, it was my turn to enter the boxing ring, my new pals from the Essex Regiment were giving me a warm welcome.

The referee blew his whistle and I could immediately see that my opponent was quite good and I knew I had a fight on my hands. He proceeded to throw a series of hard punches most of which I managed to avoid. I must admit I enjoyed this fight even though I took some punishment but I like to think he took some from me in return. The judges voted that it was the best fight in the competition between two evenly matched boxers. To my surprise, it was decided that

I was the winner on points, but in all honesty the decision could have gone either way.

The satisfaction of competing in and winning that boxing match pleased me immensely. There were three reasons why it felt so good to win. Firstly, I'd proved to those Essex boys that I really could box and that I'd earnt their respect. Secondly, I had stood up to be counted in regard to the thieves who had stolen much of my army kit. I knew they would never steal any of my kit again because of my success in the boxing ring. Thirdly, the situation I found myself in was very similar to the Sergeant Davis escapade at Quebec Barracks. I had to prove I was no pushover. (Shame on those to whom I had to prove myself to in the boxing ring once more.)

"Only our individual faith in freedom can keep us free."

Dwight D. Eisenhower.

18

Visibly Shaken in Ceylon

The boxing match had taken place on the Indian Ocean, having left the Bay of Bengal where I can remember a lovely breeze coming in from the sea, which really was a change from the Red Sea. If we had held the boxing tournament there in that excruciating heat, goodness knows what would have happened.

Our next port of call was Colombo in Ceylon (now Sri Lanka). It is a very small island shaped like a teardrop, which lies at the southern most tip of India on the East Coast of the country. At one time this was ruled by the British Empire. I can clearly remember my mother would go into raptures over Ceylon Tea, saying that, "Ceylon Tea is the best of all the cups of tea that I have ever tasted." It is strange that one can remember certain things that our parents would have told us years ago. I can vouch that my mother was absolutely right after drinking cups of Ceylon tea myself when in Ceylon.

Colombo, the capital of Ceylon, was a hive of activity. I visited when we were given a days shore leave. It was a Third World country and after just one day I was visibly shaken by what I saw. It was in Colombo that I saw the hustle and bustle of an overcrowded city of massive proportion. There, I became aware of the hardship suffered by the lower caste people in their thousands. I saw them wandering the streets begging, which I had never seen on such a scale before.

The children were begging and pleading, some with tears in their eyes. The ghastly caste system, of which India and Sri Lanka are part of, is divided up into three castes. These are the Higher Caste, the Middle Caste and the Lower Caste. Eighty percent of the population are in the Lower Caste, who generally have an absolutely horrifying life. Whereas, the Higher Caste make millions off the backs of the Lower Caste, women and children are discriminated against quite dreadfully.

In recent years (2000's), Sri Lanka has become a popular destination for British tourists with its beautiful and popular beaches. Whereas during my visit there, British holiday makers would never have even contemplated travelling such as distance for a holiday, which they could ill afford, generally they would settle for the nearest seaside town in the UK - how times have changed.

After my one day's leave in Ceylon, the Dilwara set sail once again for another long voyage, this time to Singapore, which meant more lying in the sun, where I was beginning to get slightly bored. Our troopship passed through the Bay of Bengal and finally the Dilwara had entered the Johor Strait, which had become an important shipping lane for ships going in and out of the Port of Singapore.

19

Singapore

As I stood watching from the top deck of the Dilwara, I had a spectacular view of the island of Singapore, and I remembered that just under twenty years previous the Japanese had invaded Singapore. I have always had an interest in all the countries I've visited in the Army but it was undoubtedly Singapore which created most interest for me. Primarily because I wondered how on earth had the Japanese managed to invade Singapore in the Second World War. Singapore defended itself with big guns facing the sea, in the event that a hostile force would come from that direction.

In 1938, the British had built the biggest Far East Naval Base, which had been hailed as an impregnable garrison. It was regarded as being highly unlikely to fall because of the scale of fortification.

However, the Japanese completely fooled the British by not attacking from the sea, but chose to enter via Malaya in the North and with great speed, with its marauding troops killing all before them. The British did not offer too much resistance and were unable to stop the Japanese charge. The fall of Singapore came quickly. On the 15th February 1942, came the surrender of Singapore, which was one of the greatest and humiliating defeats Britain had ever suffered in its history. The Japanese by this time were committing the most gruesome atrocities imaginable and gave British soldiers hell if they were taken as prisoners of war. They then suffered inhuman treatment to say the least. The British Prime Minister, Winston Churchill, was visibly shocked when he remarked,

"It never occurred to me for one single moment that the Great Fortress of Singapore would fall."

The Japanese held Singapore for just over three and a half years along with Malaya, Sumatra and Java. Many other areas in South East Asia were left exposed to the Japanese. At that time, a lot of these small islands would have nothing with which to defend themselves. On the 15th August 1945, the Japanese surrendered and all the Far East would be free from the Japanese domination. Great Britain and its Allies brought back peace and stability to all areas of conflict where many thousands had lost their lives.

On reaching Singapore we had been informed that the troopship Dilwara would not be proceeding any further than Singapore. It meant that the soldiers of the Essex Regiment and soldiers of other regiments would have to wait a further three weeks for another troopship to arrive and take us for the remainder of our journey to Hong Kong. What was disappointing was that we wouldn't be staying in Singapore, which was beginning to look like a very attractive place to stay, as I am sure it would have lots of entertainment and places to visit and explore. We had been told that we were being sent to a place called Nee Soon, which was about fifteen miles North from Singapore, where we would be stationed at a transit camp. I'm sure I speak for all those Essex boys that our spirits may have sank somewhat to be stuck in a transit camp, miles from anywhere. However, those early fears on going to Nee Soon never materialised.

The stay turned out to be a very pleasant three weeks even though we slept in canvas-type tents. We were more than comfortable and providing we kept ourselves clean and presentable at the daily Muster Parade everything was fine. Nee Soon looked more like a small town than a village and seemed to cater for everyone visiting there. We played plenty of football and we were always occupied. Every day we visited the swimming pool because of the hot temperatures.

The Essex Boys were all regular attenders of the cinema, which was full of soldiers and virtually all were smokers. Now, being a non-smoker, I fully understand why non-smokers couldn't use that cinema, because the smoke was excessive. The place was full of thick heavy smoke and it is not unreasonable to think that if a lighted cigarette was dropped to the floor that the whole place would have gone up in flames. I did eventually stop smoking at the age of forty-two which is probably one of the better things I've done in my life.

"Word to the Nation:
Guard zealously your right to
serve in the Armed Forces,
for without them,
there will be no other rights to guard."

President John F. Kennedy.

20

Arrival in Hong Kong

After spending three weeks in Nee Soon, it was time to move back to Singapore and await the troopship. This ship would take all the soldiers of the Essex Regiment and servicemen from other regiments to our final destination, the British colony of Hong Kong. This leg of the journey was going to be another fifteen hundred miles, when we would sail on the South China Seas in the troopship Empire Clyde. While we were aboard this ship it was very pleasant to be told there would be no more troop decks to sleep in and there would only be five soldiers to a cabin. Hearing this news made us absolutely ecstatic, as sleeping on the Dilwara's troop decks was near impossible. There had been a distinct lack of privacy with many disturbing interruptions that carried on throughout the night.

On boarding the Empire Clyde it was most noticeable that there wasn't the number of soldiers on board, as many had disembarked at Singapore. It was more satisfying that we could walk around the ship without bumping in to anyone.

Brief History of the Empire Clyde

The Empire Clyde was built in 1920 and was owned by the Anchor Line in Glasgow. She had started her life as a passenger liner named Cameronia and in 1941, the liner was requisitioned as a troopship for the Second World War. In 1953, she was renamed the Empire Clyde where she continued to be used as a troopship by the Ministry of Transport. Finally in the year 1957, the Empire Clyde was scrapped at Newport. Although this ship probably didn't have such a good war record as the Dilwara, the meals in the cookhouse were excellent. (The Dilwara's could be very ordinary at times!)

H.M.T. EMPIRE CLYDE

The Troopship H.M. Empire Clyde.

I haven't got a clue of the date or time that the Empire Clyde left Singapore but at a rough guess it would be at the end of September. All I do remember is it was daylight when I got my first glimpse of Hong Kong. I'll never forget it. I was already thinking, 'What a glorious place to be doing my National Service.'As we approached Hong Kong in our troopship from the West, I was struck by the awesome beauty of the magnificent Victoria Harbour, especially where the harbour separates Kowloon on the mainland from Hong Kong Island itself. (One is never likely to find anywhere else the same in the world.)

As I write, now sixty years later about my first sight of Hong Kong, I realise that over a period of sixty years enormous changes have taken place since I was there as a soldier. Today if I was to visit Hong Kong, I'm sure it has altered out of all proportion that I wouldn't recognise the Hong Kong I once knew. Although, what wouldn't have altered would be the harbour where the port would be full of ships of all sizes going about their business. I can well remember the hills of Hong Kong Island. There were many luxurious high-rise flats being built, all of them were facing the harbour offering up its magnificent view. According to reports from friends who have visited Hong Kong Island recently, those high-rise flats have been replaced by endless skyscrapers reaching for the sky. There is nothing to compare with the impact of Hong Kong Island; its appearance is as if a second New York City has been built there.

In the middle of the 1950s, this small British Colony really was the pride and joy of British capitalism, and the success proved to be a revelation. In those days the population of Hong Kong would be roughly

Room mates - All great blokes - Essex Regiment in B Company.

The author wearing the Summer uniform of the Essex Regiment.
The old tin roofed huts accommodated the Regiment.
It was baking hot weather with intense heat.

about five million people, which would be spread out across 425 square miles. As the whole area was growing rapidly, and Hong Kong had become one of the world's greatest population densities with the city of Kowloon being the peninsula with many thousands of people living there. Much of Hong Kong's population would be of Chinese descent, with immigrants coming in from all over China in order to contribute to Hong Kong's success.

The immigrants have undoubtedly achieved so much for Hong Kong's prosperity proving to be flourishing business people of creativity and potential. Hong Kong today has a population of over seven million people and the place seems to be bulging at the seams with shoppers because of the massive expansion of people. There has been the construction of massive residential blocks of buildings and in the New Territories of the north of Kowloon have now become cities which originally were villages. The Chinese immigrants are often described as hard working and the success of Hong Kong can be accredited to their tenacity and willingness to work hard (long may their success continue).

The headquarters of the 2nd Battalion of the Essex Regiment in Hong Kong was situated in Natham Road, Kowloon where we stayed for just a couple of days after disembarking from our troopship Empire Clyde. While there we had even more inoculations to protect us against more diseases in Hong Kong. We were also kitted out with all the summer army clothes we would be wearing in the excessively hot temperatures at that time of year.

Good Soldier

And make no mistake about it. Tommy Atkins here is a very good soldier indeed. He is superbly fit. His morale generally is very high. He is as keen on his job as any soldier can be while not actually employed in an active role.

Out near the China border, where dead - pan Communist soldiers stare stolidly across the few feet of no-man's-land, I visited the 1st Battalion of the Essex Regiment, which came here straight from Korea. It is recognised as a crack unit but that, to its great credit, is strictly in spite of circumstances.

The men of Essex are living in patched-up old tin-roofed huts which brew up to a cruel temperature in the intense heat of the Summer days here and do not cool off quickly at night.

Maybe one day—given just a little extra cash, of which there seems to be such a plentiful supply in this part of the world— shortcomings like these will be put right.

But morally it will still be up to the people of Hongkong to make Tommy Atkins feel less of a stranger in their paradise.

They could do that to-morrow— if they wanted to.

London newspaper cutting (1956)
reporting on the Regiment's living conditions.

We were told at a meeting that we had to immediately report to Fanling, in the New Territories of Hong Kong, just fifteen miles north of Kowloon and close to the border of Communist China. It was in Fanling that B Company of the Essex Regiment was stationed. We were required to patrol the border at regular intervals with help from other regiments.

I think all of us who were new to Hong Kong were disappointed that we were leaving Kowloon so very quickly, as we agreed that it would have been so exciting to have seen all that the city offered, and once we were up in the New Territories it would perhaps be difficult to contemplate a reason for visiting Kowloon. So it was, that many soldiers from the Essex Regiment including many of the ex-Northamptonshire boys travelled by train into the wilds of the New Territories not knowing what to expect. We knew if China's troops stayed on their side of the border then not one shot would be fired.

I was slightly apprehensive about the border line between Hong Kong and China, would our defences be adequate to stop a Chinese charge, where British troops would have been greatly outnumbered. China had always maintained Hong Kong should be part of their country - would she be patient to last out the 99 Year Lease and then claim the territory back without opposition from the British Government? I'm sure none of the residents of Hong Kong would want to revert back as they thrived under British rule.

'B' Company - Essex Regiment travelling by train from Fanling to Kowloon for yet another Army Parade. The author remembers being packed in like

21

The New Territories

Just two days after arriving in Hong Kong on the Empire Clyde the Essex boys found themselves at the southern end of Kowloon, near Victoria Harbour in order to catch a train at the Hung Hom railway station bound for the New Territories. This area was known to be one of the most populated places on earth making up more than 90% of Hong Kong's land, where it was known as the New Territories. The 40 minute train journey would take us to the small town of Fanling where soldiers of the 2nd Battalion of the Essex Regiment have been stationed for many years. A short distance away was Communist China's border with Hong Kong, near to Shenzhen, and then the vastness of China where their troops wouldn't be far away.

While travelling on a train, it really came home to me, as I sat and contemplated the scenery, that riding in a train carriage is the best way possible of seeing places like Kowloon and the New Territories. (I wouldn't necessarily have seen them if I had been driving a car.) To look through a railway carriage window on leaving Kowloon was an absolute delight. I saw Kowloon briefly, it looked like a vibrant and exciting city in the New Territories. Fanling, in particular, filled me with optimism and hope. Les my best friend was with me, we had one another to rely on as the hard times would invariably come our way. The next twelve months would be crucial and England and my family really did seem a million miles away.

If I was to give the impression that serving the British Army overseas was a cushy experience in comparison to serving one's National Service in Great Britain one couldn't be more wrong. In many respects it was harder being a soldier abroad.

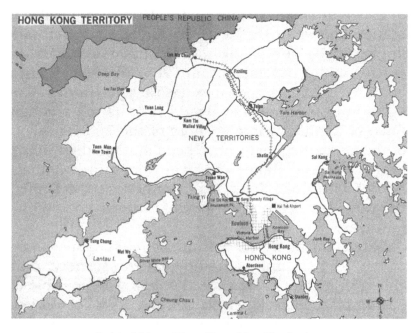

Original Map - Hong Kong New Territories.

In Hong Kong we had to be very much aware of what could seriously happen if China decided to invade Hong Kong. The Communist border of China was just three miles from Fanling, and because of what China's troops were capable of, if they crossed the border in their thousands, which would easily outnumber the small contingent of British soldiers stationed in the New Territories, soldiers had to be superbly fit.

The Cenotaph in Kowloon where
'B' Company of the Essex Regiment
would be on parade
on Remembrance Sunday.

The bull I experienced at Quebec Barracks in Northampton during my training was definitely portrayed in the Essex Regiment. We had to be out of our beds by 6.30am, when it was a case of a quick wash and shave and often running to the cookhouse in order not to miss breakfast. We would stand by our beds for our Platoon Sergeant Shepherd, who would then inspect them and criticize us for any speck of dust or dirt found under the bed or behind the cupboards. Then the whole of B Company would attend the Muster Parade on the Drill Square for the daily morning inspection of our dress. We would invariably go on a twenty mile route march or spend an hour or so square bashing.

Essex Regiment on parade in Kowloon.

Yes, square bashing was very much part of infantry life and in the fourteen months that I spent in Hong Kong we would rehearse every day for some parade or other.

One parade I can distinctly remember was performing in one of Kowloon's biggest football stadiums. In front of thirty thousand spectators, the Essex Regiment was involved in the opening ceremony of a military tattoo. Marching around the stadium, to much applause with the flag of the Essex Regiment flowing magnificently in the breeze, we saluted the Governor of Hong Kong. At the finish of the evening 'God Save the Queen' was sung. The whole evening had been marvellous with a terrific atmosphere. I can also remember that same squad of soldiers performing at the Queen's Birthday celebrations.

2nd Battalion Essex Regiment - Army Evening Parade.

The author on Parade.

2nd Battalion Essex Regiment - Army Parade.

We marched through the streets of Kowloon again with much applause from the crowds on the pavements, paying our respects on Remembrance Sunday at the memorial in Kowloon.

The Essex Regiment gave a public display of homage for the suffering Kowloon residents endured during the three years invasion by Japanese troops. There were other parades but none as significant as these. On thinking back over those days, especially the Tattoo, I'm sure all the soldiers who performed so well felt they had achieved something very special. I know I felt that way and I was proud to be an Essex soldier, so many of those Essex boys had become good friends of mine.

GIBRALTAR— IN HONG KONG

Under searchlights, the Essex and Northamptonshire Regiments parade in the New Territories of Hong Kong.

TWO non-existent battalions have celebrated their bicentenaries in Hong Kong; the 2nd Battalion The Essex Regiment and the 2nd Battalion The Northamptonshire Regiment.

Both went into suspended animation in 1947. For this important anniversary, the 1st Battalions of each regiment, stationed in Hong Kong, were allowed to assume the titles of their second battalions.

The parade was staged at night at San Wai, Fanling, in the New Territories, under the searchlights of a movement troop, Royal Artillery. Those present included Sir Alexander Grantham, the Governor of Hong Kong, and Lieutenant-General Sir Cecil Sugden, commanding British Forces in Hong Kong.

An impressive backcloth showed the Castle of Gibraltar, the emblem awarded to both regiments for their part in the defence of the Rock in the great siege.

The 2nd Battalion The Essex Regiment were formerly the 56th of Foot and were known as "The Pompadours." That name derived ... their facings— "rose-

pompadour," the favourite colour of Madame de Pompadour, mistress of Louis XV.

The 2nd Battalion The Northamptonshire Regiment were formerly the 58th. The Colours carried on this parade were presented in 1860, and are among the very few remaining sets of Colours of the old dimensions—five feet flying, and four feet six inches to the pike. The pikes are surmounted by spearheads instead of crowns.

They are believed to be the last Colours in present-day use to have been carried in action—at the Battle of Laing's Nek, in 1881.

At the Royal Review at Aldershot in 1935 King George V directed that these Colours, because of their age, would not be flown during the march-past. Now, on all occasions, the Colours are held to the pikes.

To commemorate the battle honour "Gibraltar" the parade fired a feu-de-joie, a salute permitted only on the Sovereign's birthday or in recognition of a notable victory.—From a report by Major K. C. Harvey, Army Public Relations.

The main Army Parades of the 2nd Battalion The Essex Regiment.

22

Guard Duties and Route Marches

At the army camp in Fanling, every soldier in the Essex Regiment would have responsibility of doing night time guard duties, approximately every three weeks. In pairs, we would patrol the whole of the camp area particularly at night time as it was felt that anything was likely to happen. There was always a possibility that someone would break into the camp by cutting through the eight foot high wire fence, which surrounded the whole of the army camp area.

Once I came off Guard duties, a large hole had been found in the fence and the six guardsmen on duty that night, myself included, were sent for by the Commanding Officer of B Company. He was none too pleased and wanted to know if we had been asleep all night, to which we answered most emphatically "No Sir". He just couldn't understand why we hadn't seen the large hole in the fence. He then went on to say that if damage had been done in the camp or even worse if a bomb had been found, we would be in serious trouble for not reporting such an incident.

We were fortunate, our Commanding Officer Major O'Reilly, who was well liked and respected by all the soldiers in B Company took our word for the damaged fence. We fully expected to be put on a charge, but the overriding question remained, had someone managed to get into our Army Camp or had someone managed to get out of our Army Camp? This incident managed to remain a complete mystery.

Never did I envisage the effect of so much square bashing and its continued effect on my life. When I reached the age of fifty-three I would once again indulge in my love of serious walking by entering many marathons. My passion for walking came from my time stationed in Hong Kong. You see, I actually enjoyed the regular route marches. Some days we

Getting ready for the Field Exercises.

94

would walk twenty miles in full Battle Dress as we had to be prepared for the likelihood of going into battle. I know those route marches didn't seem to take much out of me, as when we returned to our camp just about everyone would be lying on their beds in total exhaustion, and although I was obviously very tired, I had relished every stride I had taken.

I have never forgotten those route marches where we would march down many a country road and pass through small villages. Often we were met with much applause, it was the locals' way of saying they appreciated the British Army being there. I also believe those route marches along with all the other physical exercises we indulged in always kept me in good health and my weight never went above ten stone.

I never forgot that we were in Hong Kong for a purpose and I believe that all the soldiers in the New Territories were reasonably well trained, but we were never put to the ultimate test, thank goodness. Still, all those route marches were absolutely essential to reach peak physical fitness as the enemy, at any particular time, might venture over the border. We had to be in a permanent state of readiness as much as we could possibly be.

If some of B Company's soldiers thought the route marches were tough then the Army field exercises were much tougher. For these we had to run up Hong Kong's hills in full battle dress. At the Muster Parade on those mornings it was necessary to include equipment like shovels and crowbars to dig trenches. Nearly all of the soldiers of the Essex Regiment A, B and C Companies would be involved along with the soldiers from other infantry regiments partaking in the exercise. We would be taken in army lorries to a very remote part of the New Territories. Here we would indulge in fighting the enemy, not that there would be a real enemy as it was only a practice of the real thing, but it was really confusing as the enemy was never seen.

Using tanks in training.

23

Field Exercises in the New Territories

The daily transaction of digging, sleeping and eating in the trenches definitely portrayed a war-like atmosphere that could only be found in a battlefield somewhere. The army field exercises could only give an indication of the happenings of the real thing as no weapons, rifles or grenades were used. These exercises would be as near as possible to the real thing but only friendly fire was used.

The army field exercises would last at least a week and I can clearly remember one incident that will never leave me in view of the seriousness of what could have happened! In a squad of a dozen soldiers, we were retreating further and further up a slight hill as the enemy was supposedly gaining ground on us, but as there was no real enemy to be seen it was left to the non-commissioned officers. These being the Sergeant Majors who were supposed to be informing us of the enemy's position.

A gravestone found in the hills of the
New Territories.

Climbing mountains in full battle dress.
Hot weather made it very tiring.

One soldier in our squad thought he heard an order to fire to our right. With this information we fired on the enemy to the right of where we were, although of course, there was no enemy to be seen. We then had the satisfaction we had 'seen off the enemy' with the squad being jubilant as to what we had achieved but, I have to write, we were not jubilant for long.

We were soon brought down to earth, our squad by firing to the right had killed our own soldiers. I can only offer a feeble excuse with all the noise going on, genuine messages do not always get through, and my sympathy goes to that lone soldier who thought he had heard correctly but evidently he hadn't.

Trench Digging. The author in centre sitting with Les.

It really was very confusing. There was always a lesson in life to be learned from this incident and one should never attack the enemy unless the

99

Digging trenches in the New Territories.

Mountain terrain.

Platoon Officer has been wounded and unable to assume command. If he cannot give the orders then a junior officer or a platoon sergeant would take over. In the heat of the battle mistakes do happen and if that dreadful incident was done in a real life battle situation we would be guilty of killing our own men. (How on earth would we have lived with that?) At our army camp in Fanling, both Les and myself found ourselves settling into B Company. By then we had quickly realised that we had to contend with the sweltering heat, we would never have experienced at home in Great Britain. Life being so different that at a particular time we would finish whatever activity in which we were involved, in order to have lunch at 1pm. We were encouraged to rest when the scorching heat was at its most powerful.

This invariably meant dropping off to sleep on our beds. By 5pm we would carry on with what we previously had been doing as the weather became increasingly cooler for an evening's work. We did not forget the evening meal in the cookhouse, which was not to be missed.

While sleeping in the afternoon, there was never any possibility of putting one's mosquito net over your bed, but at night time, in those tin-roofed Nissan huts where we slept, every soldier had a mosquito net to cover his bed. In the darkness of the night, these blood-sucking, flying insects were rampant; buzzing around our nets like noisy spitfires, trying to attack each soldier. Without the protection of those nets, goodness knows what could have happened, receiving a mosquito bite would be very serious indeed. Yet, when daylight appeared those 'spitfires' had disappeared completely only to try to attack its

The boys relaxing after a long day on the

Getting down for a night's sleep.

prey again the following night. If there were a hole in the net, the mosquito was sure to find it and then the soldier would go berserk trying to find this invader in the dark and consequently waking up all the soldiers in the Nissan hut. How difficult it was trying to find just one mosquito. This was one of the many hazards on being a British soldier in Hong Kong.

It was not easy for any Westerner, myself included, to see a country full of poverty. It was seeing people blind, crippled and paralysed begging on the streets in Hong Kong, which left me in a state of uneasiness. It was in Kowloon, and then Fanling, that I was most aware of the situation, but probably because of being a teenager I was not affected like I thought I would be, in seeing a different world and a way of life that didn't exist in my own country.

I now believe, on reflection, I should have been more prepared for what I was about to experience in the Far East, particularly in Hong Kong. Not that the poverty was on a scale of what I saw many years later in India; or for that matter, what I'd seen in Ceylon just a few weeks earlier. Perhaps the poverty I was about to witness was due to my own incompetence by not reading of the subject before I set sail from Southampton.

I really should have learned about the country where I was to spend fourteen months, but being in my teens then I could quite easily dismiss all the poverty I was to see by thinking it was certainly not my problem. I now realise I was selfish to even think such a thing. But when we are young we sometimes say or do things without thinking of the consequences of our actions and I was no different in that respect than any other young man of my age.

Paddy fields in the New Territories.

I was indeed privileged to be born to the very best of parents where I was well loved and wanted. My parents never put me on the streets at the age of four to go begging. Yet if I had been born in a slum area of Hong Kong many years ago, in all probability that would have happened to me, but by the flick of a coin either heads or tails, I came up trumps. I've always realised how fortunate I've been and I have got a lot to thank God for.

The Essex Regiment and other regiments were greatly involved in keeping the security between the New Territories in the North of Hong Kong and the vastness of Communist China.

There were two villages entangled in keeping the peace; the village of Low Wai in the New Territories, and the village of Shenzhen in China. This was where the border line was split right through the middle of the two villages. In between the villages there was a small river, not much wider than a country lane, where there was also a high barbed wire fence. It had been erected by the British in order to keep out China's thousands of refugees from crossing the border into the New Territories.

To maintain tight security, there was a twenty four hour watch duty, every minute, every hour, every day and every night over a period of many years on the Low Wai side of the border involving several regiments from Great Britain.

I know that there have been many skirmishes over the years with refugees trying to cross over the border but I can't recall the Essex Regiment when I was there having any trouble of that nature.

Occasionally we would see the soldiers of Communist China who would be patrolling on their side of the border. They would solemnly stare at us across the few yards of 'No Man's Land' to our side of the border. We would often wave as a friendly gesture, but this was rarely returned. Our troops had tried to be sociable but it just never happened.

I have written previously about the Japanese attack on Singapore, which fell on the 15th February 1942. Now I write about the capitulation of Hong Kong on the 25th December 1941, which took place just under 20 years before my arrival in Hong Kong. I couldn't help but listen and learn about the inhumane treatment of prisoners, where the Japanese neither had the time or the inclination to treat their prisoners of war with care and humanity. Prisoners were just killed and slaughtered in a most barbaric way.

The Japanese committed appalling atrocities against helpless and defenceless people. I would rather not write anything that would distress anyone, but I have to say their crimes were absolutely horrendous. Why were the Japanese so cruel in wartime? It is incongruous to me as the few Japanese people I've ever met seem gentle and kind people who would never show any signs of aggression.

The mountain terrain.

24

A Dear John Letter

Have you ever heard of a 'Dear John' letter? Receiving one can be soul destroying to the receiver of such a letter, as any serving young soldier serving in the British Army abroad will tell you. It really was one of the worst experiences a young soldier is ever likely to have. When receiving a 'Dear John' letter from his girlfriend back home in Great Britain there was always a touch of humour in the barrack room if it became known that one such soldier had received such a letter. I myself always felt very sympathetic for any soldier caught up in this horrid situation, where the soldier concerned is totally devastated.

A soldier's ultimate joy was to receive his girlfriend's letter once a week or in sometimes every day. For many soldiers, to receive his girlfriend's letter made Army life bearable. The letter confirmed how much she loved him and was counting the days, weeks and months when her soldier arrived home again and they could talk about their marriage plans together.

Try to imagine a young soldier in Hong Kong or any other overseas posting, after having a bad day with the square bashing, was then cheered up enormously on seeing the letter from his darling girlfriend. He opens the letter excitedly. On reading the letter he is brought down to earth with a big bang, aghast with his girlfriend's letter and in his confused state can't understand what is happening. He is completely demoralised with what he reads, she has met someone else and the relationship with her soldier boyfriend must end.

"But what happened? I thought she loved me." He asks himself. This is what happened as many servicemen abroad may have received a 'Dear John' letter. The soldier I refer to remained absolutely shattered for many weeks afterwards and seemed to lose much confidence as he had relied so much on his girlfriend's letters. From then onwards he was a very unhappy man. As regards myself, I can remember writing to one ex-girlfriend, just once, as I didn't want that extra responsibility of having a regular girlfriend because long separations do not always make a relationship last.

I can recall my friend Les, writing to his girlfriend every single day, then marrying her when he was demobbed. However, a few years later the marriage failed and I wonder if Les were here today would he have done anything differently? Knowing Les the way he was, he would probably answer, *"Yes, definitely, I must have spent an absolute fortune on writing paper, envelopes and stamps literally every day, and I know now why I was always broke."* He may have added, *"What a fool and waste it all was, as half of the time in Hong Kong I was writing letters to my girlfriend instead of enjoying myself."* Then with a smile on his face he would have remarked, *"Perhaps I should have received a 'Dear John' myself as it would have solved many of the problems I was to experience later in my marriage."*

The Hong Kong I shall always remember is of the glorious days of endless sunshine when on waking up every morning I was greeted by another beautiful day. However, there is often two sides to every story... when it rains, like it invariably did in Hong Kong, (any storm damage usually happened at night), nervous looking soldiers, myself included, would lie on our beds being full of anticipation by what might occur. We would worry whether those patched-up, tin roofed huts we lived in would survive another night. Those gale force winds created a creaky and clattery sound throughout the night which became more evident as time progressed with the ceilings looking very vulnerable indeed. We thought our huts might literally cave in at any time.

As all huts were identical, we all experienced the same problem: leakage in most huts, with never-ending flashes of lightning during a thunder storm and ferocious winds.

At the Fanling Army Camp one of the huts was used as an ammunition hut. This was situated well away from all the other tin huts. The soldiers were warned never to smoke near this particular hut as just a spark would cause a massive explosion.

Yes, those dreadful nights we experienced in our huts could be very frightening, with the possibility of a soldier more likely to be killed from a crashed-down ceiling than to be killed by a communist soldier's bullet!

*"I just put my feet in the air
and move them around."*

Fred Astaire.

25

My Strictly (I'm No Fred Astaire!)

Some evenings, with Les and a few others in our camp, we would take a ten minute stroll into the shopping area of the Fanling town centre. The shop keepers were at times desperate for business to be done and just occasionally we would be able to barter them down. If they had a poor day the products they were selling in the clothing department or whatever, appealed to the buyer then business could be achieved providing one had sufficient money with them of course, on obtaining the reduced price. We would then be offered a cup of tea or if they were of a more generous nature something stronger.

Those shopkeepers would recognize an Englishman straight away, even in civilian clothes, which we were allowed to wear in the evenings. I think the local people tolerated us in view of the simple fact we were there for their benefit. In the vicinity, was a cinema, which seemed to be used by most of the British soldiers in the New Territories. Many evenings it would be a full house. Every other evening it was a film that had just been released. I know Les and I were regular attenders at this cinema, sometimes going twice a week. It was always good entertainment and not to be missed. We had only been in Fanling a few months when I was to discover there were a couple of dance halls in the town and I persuaded Les to come with me to see what it would be really like.

It was a Saturday night in Fanling, I automatically thought of my home town of Peterborough. When I was a teenager, Saturday night was always the big night out of the week. On finding one of the dance halls, Les refused to enter and I believe he was showing loyalty to his girlfriend for which I admired him tremendously.

The town of Fanling in the New Territories.

Once in the Hall, I was told there was no admission fee but for every dance there would be a small charge. On sitting down in this dimly-lit hall I noticed six, young, teenage Chinese girls who seemed to be full of curiosity and were smiling broadly at me from the other side of the dance floor. I found this very odd as there was no dancing going on. It was then that something crossed my mind that maybe I was in a place of ill repute. Could this be the reason? And what should I do next? I thought.

As one of those attractive young girls came walking towards me, I became anxious as to what sort of impertinent question this girl was about to ask me. Fortunately to suffer any embarrassment on my part I was very much relieved when she asked me to dance with her. She was a brilliant dancer, as were all the other girls. For the hour I spent with her the charge was 25p which I suppose looking back was a really low, ridiculous figure.

All the girls working at the dance hall would be country girls from poor families who would have come in to the town and would have no qualifications whatsoever. From then onwards I would attend that dance hall quite often. I was never in the category of a Fred Astaire but during that time my dancing showed a big improvement, I had found, 'Strictly Come Dancing' in Hong Kong and I loved it.

A dance hall girl, who married one of our soldiers, must have had a huge culture shock when she moved to the UK. A huge difference of appalling poverty, living in mud huts to comparative luxury back in England – we have many advantages of which we take for granted.

Camping in the wilds of the New Territories -
the author is in there somewhere!

Digging trenches in the sweltering heat was extremely hot work
with not one shirt on!

I can't remember too many of their names but I'll never forget them.

What a great picture this is of some of the lads from 'B' Company,
it would make a great bonding session.

26

Camaraderie in the Field

The army field exercises, which the Essex Regiment would be involved in, would happen about every three months and I found myself on guard duties with many others. In twos we would patrol a very large area, which took in the hills of the New Territories. As we surveyed the most illustrious landscape, where at night time, in the distance (less than two miles away) we could see the lights of Communist China. In the winter months it was very cold and I would invariably think of my family at home.

Once again I would feel a million miles away from my loved ones because in those days Hong Kong would just about be the farthest of all postings possible. That winter, Great Britain was proving to be as cold as the New Territories and I would visualise all my family at home. They would be gathered round the open fire in the kitchen every evening; my mother and father along with my three brothers with their outstretched hands hanging over the open fire in order to keep warm—with the cat and the dog also sharing some of the heat. (I must point out that in the middle 1950s there was no such thing as central heating.)

Those army field exercises seemed to bring out the very best in every soldier in the Essex Regiment and I'm sure that would be the case of all British regiments over the many years stationed in Hong Kong. Those days, away from the spit and polish one would experience in an army camp or barrack room where the bull reigns supreme, out in the fields of the New Territories there was a more relaxed attitude. Every soldier in B Company was pulling his weight and not letting the side down, great comradeship had developed, particularly when there was work to be done like digging trenches there was always plenty of helpers, many volunteers willingly stepped forward.

Our Platoon Officer was Lieutenant Hutchens, who was a gentleman in every respect, was well liked by all the soldiers under him.

Winners of Fighting Patrol having blacked our faces in the

Admittedly, there was some grumbling in the ranks where some would swear like troopers, but in all fairness that was all part of army life made up of many different individuals. Sometimes we would be part of the army manoeuvres at night time, crawling about in the dark. Trying to find the enemy proved to be near impossible, but the comradeship of the Essex boys was usually very good.

Once, I recall, when I got talking to my father, who for once talked about the World War I trenches, he said, that was what saved him from going insane—the camaraderie of the British troops—without which he would have gone mad! Call it what you like, camaraderie, comradeship or team spirit, I always found plenty in abundance in the Essex Regiment, which was what my father meant when he was in the trenches. I always found that those Cockney East Enders always had a great sense of humour and would crack a joke whilst digging the deepest of trenches (with the mandatory swear word of course).

The photograph gives a fair indication of eight soldiers in training fully prepared for the enemy in a military night-time exercise as a fighting patrol. We were appropriately dressed for such an occasion, equipped with the necessary firearms. The night happened to be one of the worst nights one can imagine - with torrential rain while we crawled on our knees in the mud. In reality, during a real war-like situation, this could be the case irrespective of the weather.

The two sides of being a soldier in Hong Kong. To enjoy the beaches (less than three miles from Fanling, to the spit and polish of all the bull in the barrack room.

The Golden Sands of the New Territories where the Essex Troops would make for whenever they could.

Ted Towel and me.
Duties included Bulling Up, it was all spit and polish with mosquito net being ready for bed.

27

Sport — My Saviour

During my time in Hong Kong I played plenty of sports, not just by being involved in football, boxing, swimming and walking but occasionally indoor sports such as table tennis and snooker. As regards football, I was picked regularly to play for the B Company football team, which I enjoyed immensely. There were times it could be an advantage being a footballer.

At the daily Muster Parade, all the footballers who had been selected to play football for B Company that afternoon were subsequently excused of all that day's duties and dismissed in preparation for the football match. On being excused, we were allowed to return to our barrack rooms to relax in a certain manner—not exerting oneself in any way. Relieved of such duties, meant that we could well be missing out on more square bashing or some other arduous task. So all the footballers of B Company were determined to keep their places safe in the football team (providing of course that we continued winning).

Although, I was a regular member of 'B' Company Football Team I can never remember a photograph ever being taken of the team. However, just occasionally a game would be played between barrack rooms. The matches were not taken too seriously as the photograph shows as we never had the proper football clothes like shirts and shorts etc but we still enjoyed it. This particular game was played at the Northamptonshire Regiment's Sports Field where a board in the background of the photograph is seen. I knew one of the Northamptonshire Team players who came from Peterborough where we had a good old chin wag abut the army, both the good and the bad.

The only photograph of the author playing football in Hong Kong.

During the excessive hot weather in the Hong Kong summertime, on having been given the afternoon off, many of us caught the big army truck. It would take any soldier who was interested in swimming, to the beach, which would enable us to swim in the sea.

The beach was only about three miles from Fanling. There really were some beautiful beaches all over Hong Kong and probably more so, in the New Territories with miles and miles of endless sandy white beaches. They were often unoccupied with no other swimmer to be seen. Swimming in the lovely warm sea and lying on those beaches was marvellous in the hot sun and was an amazing benefit of serving as a soldier in Her Majesty's Forces.

I did manage to have one last boxing match against a boxer who gave me a real beating. As I have mentioned before one never knows in the army about ones opponent and in this boxing match he was far superior to me in the boxing ring. I took a lot of punishment with the referee stopping the fight in the second round. I think boxing is very much a great experience when you are winning but completely different when you are losing, particularly when one is losing badly with the amount of punishment my opponent was giving me. I decided after that defeat never to box again. With the consolation being that I had won four out of five of my boxing bouts in the army. (I was happy to settle for that.)

In boxing I took many blows to the head but heading a heavy football is equally destructive as professional footballers will know as many suffered brain damage in later life where fortunately it never happened to me.

A whole cooked pig will be shared
by many families in Fanling.

Several people killed in rail crash near Fanling in 1956.

28

Worrying Times

One Saturday afternoon in Hong Kong I tried to find an address of a luxurious flat which was situated amongst many other high-rise flats on Hong Kong Island. I did eventually find it after much searching and once I had found it, this particular flat, had a magnificent view overlooking the Victoria Harbour.

In a letter from my mother she wrote that a distant relative of ours lived on the Hong Kong Island and wished to meet me and would I like to visit him? Apparently this gentleman and his wife have lived and worked in Hong Kong for many years.

Unfortunately, when I finally located the high-rise apartments, I was very disappointed when I discovered that the lift was out of action and the only way to reach this flat, being on the fifteenth floor, was to walk up the stairway, which would be a challenge I hadn't bargained for. That day just happened to be an intensely hot day. On reaching the halfway point I was sweating profusely and I must have looked very slovenly indeed. This was the last thing I wanted as I was hoping to make a good impression.

I had telephoned the gentleman earlier that morning to let him know that I would be calling on him in the afternoon. When I rung the doorbell of the flat having finally made it, the front door was opened and I was greeted by two smiling faces of the man and his wife. The least I could ask was to have a quick wash and smarten myself up once more.

The gentleman immediately apologised for the lift not working and he led me into his very plush apartment, but what took my eye again was the most extraordinary view of the glorious panorama picture of the Victoria Harbour. Now seen from the fifteenth floor of this luxurious apartment home.

I was made extremely welcome and all the conversation was comparatively easy between the three of us. After eating a typical English meal, the conversation turned to how long would British troops continue to stay in Hong Kong, which of course I couldn't answer. I would remind the reader that this was 1956, this gentleman was becoming more worried concerning China as to what would happen if China crossed over the border to invade Hong Kong. He worked as a civil servant in Kowloon and was naturally worried that such a thing would be allowed to happen and would he still be employed? Or, should he return to Great Britain? He hadn't really contemplated such a move because he and his wife had such a fantastic lifestyle in Hong Kong. However, it was worrying times. For me to have spent a few hours with this charming couple, the pleasure was all mine. It was the first time I was able to hear the views of two British people actually living in Hong Kong.

29

Christmas in the Army

Without doubt one of the greatest hazards was to be in the British Forces serving abroad when one is away from family and loved ones on Christmas Day. In the case of the 2nd Battalion of the Essex Regiment all the soldiers and servicemen throughout Hong Kong would be thousands of miles away from home while serving their country. Christmas Day of course is the celebration of the birth of Jesus Christ, which had always become a day of much festivity and did bring much needed qualities of faith, hope and love wherever one might be.

I came from a Christian church-going family. It seemed very appropriate that my mother would insist that her four sons would know the full meaning of Christmas. With much loving and giving, Christmas Day would bring happiness with joyful expectation concerning the birth of Jesus. However, being stationed in Hong Kong I would spend my first ever Christmas away from home. I would be constantly thinking of my family. I admit to missing them dreadfully and naturally wished to be with them.

Strange as it was, I had never experienced such loneliness in all my life before, even though I was literally surrounded by numerous soldiers in the Fanling Army Camp.

I was absolutely sure that many soldiers on that Christmas Day would have felt exactly the same as I felt. We experienced some periods of great despondency, but we were cheered up that we had been given One day's holiday. We could have been on guard duty or working in the Cookhouse preparing the day's meals. So, we were grateful for that, as Christmas Day could have been even worse. Later that morning, the Padre addressed all the soldiers in a field next to the camp, preaching the Christmas message and then we sung Carols. It really did seem strange to be singing Christmas Carols under a hot sun and not a cold and damp winter's evening back home.

In the evening Les and I visited the NAAFI for a drink or two, proposed good health to both our families as we knew our families would certainly be thinking of us. There was no real alternative and we really tried to make the best out of such a tense situation. Just a year later we were serving our time in Germany, at least then, it wouldn't be too long before our two years National Service would be completed.

30

Not a Pretty Sight

A lmost every soldier would do it but for me I became the most embarrassed soldier in the whole of the Fanling Army Camp. I can remember the incident clearly to this day and four young Chinese girls had much excitement at my expense! In the Camp, the washroom was about three hundred yards from the tin huts we lived in, to have a shower in the evening after a scorching hot day, meant walking across the drill square where we did our square bashing. At one side of the square was a high wire fence with a road leading to Fanling less than few yards from the square.

On having my shower, I walked the same route back to the hut with just a towel covering the lower part of my body, with my arms full carrying all of my clothes that I had worn that day, which of course would be washed at a later date. (I have to say, that all the B Company soldiers on having a shower would walk back with a towel round their waist and their arms full of the clothes worn that day.) Suddenly, from halfway across the drill square, a great gust of wind blew my towel off my body and with trying to hold onto the towel, all the clothes I was carrying in my arms were spread all over the drill square. So, here I was, apart from a pair of slippers on my feet—completely starkers—like the day I was born and ready to be swallowed up with embarrassment.

On the pavement along the side of the road, these four teenage girls had seen the whole incident by looking through the wire fence. They had witnessed the whole thing, and were hysterical with laughter. Their laughter echoed in my ears as I ran around the drill square trying to pick up my towel and clothes which were scattered all over the place. Every time I bent down to pick up my towel another gust of wind would blow it away and this went on for a few minutes. Finally, I managed to pick everything up and I continued to run to the safety of my living quarters with still the girls' laughter ringing in my ears.

Back in the hut I told everyone what had happened and they also found it hilarious saying they wished they had seen it. I admit there was a funny side but I was very conscious that something like that could happen again, particularly when strong winds are about.

31

I was Never a Lackey

There were several non-commission officers in the Essex Regiment with a military rank of Sergeant, Corporal, or Lance Corporal. The latter is the lowest rank anon-commissioned officer can be. When I became a non-commissioned officer myself, promoted just three months before the Essex Regiment were to leave Hong Kong, it meant that I became a Lance Corporal. The whole exercise of achieving some authority does not carry a commission as all non-commissioned officers are appointed from the ranks.

This promotion to Lance Corporal meant going on a two weeks training course. This would involve some studying which I hated. It reminded me of my time at Stamford School where there was so much homework to be done. On completion of the training course, I had deep reservations on whether I should be a Lance Corporal or not, because of a certain amount of suspicion on my part. A Lance Corporal was often treated like a Lackey by all the other ranks in the British Army. I would be at everyone's command like a servant or hanger-on, and could even be known as a dogsbody. I had grave misgivings about what I was about to undertake.

Financially, I would be about one pound a month better off, it was abundantly clear that I wasn't doing it for the money. I was beginning to wonder whether being a non-commissioned officer would be worth all the hassle that I would undoubtedly get. I began to ask, *"What was I letting myself in for?"* It became a question I would repeatedly ask myself. I finally decided to give it a go, but I really was full of trepidation.

I was also concerned about taking on a leadership role. What qualities did I have to qualify for such as task? Previously, I preferred to lay low and not volunteer for responsibility – partly because I lacked self-confidence. However, Lieutenant Hutchings, my Platoon Officer, had no such concerns, he was convinced I had the right qualities to step up the ladder and wished me every success.

The genuine fear of becoming a lackey never materialised and I believe I was treated with respect so I couldn't have asked for more. I was still one of the boys in the tin roofed huts we lived in and I wasn't going to spoil the good team spirit by being a Lance Corporal. Maybe I was wrong but the eleven others in the hut were all good blokes but in all fairness I was the last one to put myself about in a disorderly fashion. On becoming a Lance Corporal with one stripe it would not make the slightest difference. I had won them over and I was grateful for that.

32

Farewell to Fanling

Our fourteen months in Hong Kong finished most abruptly and, if I remember correctly, we had been informed several times that we would soon be leaving Hong Kong. The Essex Regiment was undoubtedly ready for a move but no definite date had been given, but with our bags packed we were ready to go in double quick time if necessary. The new Regiment was evidently ready to take our place and was waiting in the wings in order to move to the Fanling Army Camp. I think on looking back, I did feel a touch of sadness about leaving Fanling, admittedly there had been moments when army life would test my patience but on the bright side I had many good times in the Fanling Army Camp and, not forgetting the town of Fanling itself. But what outweighed everything was the real significance of going home.

If there was one person who I felt desperately sorry for at the Fanling Camp it was our tea boy, George, who was allowed to enter our camp every evening to sell his cooked food. The smell from his cooking, and to eat what he was selling, was very appetising indeed. When he knew we were leaving he was very despondent, he had managed to scrape a living for his wife and children and he relied on the soldiers in the Fanling Camp to buy his food at a reduced price. His hot meat rolls were certainly more edible than what was being sold in the NAAFI. George's biggest worry was that the new regiment who would take our place would not let him continue to enter the camp. In all probability it would be the Commanding Officer of the new Regiment to decide whether he would grant permission for George to still enter and sell his scrumptious homemade cooking. I have a photograph of George kneeling down in front of the soldiers of B Company where he was so very much appreciated by all the soldiers of the Essex Regiment.

Tea Boy George.

The whole regiment left Fanling by train to reach Kowloon and stayed at the barracks in Natham Road for a couple of days. During those two days we were allowed to wander around Kowloon and on the third day we would be boarding a ship home.

The ferry which takes passengers from Kowloon to Hong Kong Island.

On looking around Kowloon, it really was a beautiful city and the real disappointment of the whole time spent in Hong Kong was that because of our low wages we just couldn't afford to visit Kowloon preferring to stay in Fanling, although we would often visit Kowloon to put on a Military Parade. However, to spend time anywhere that was really out of the question. So, after the Muster Parade on those two mornings, Les and I were determined to see as much of Kowloon as possible.

First of all, we caught the early morning ferry across Victoria Harbour to the Hong Kong Island. We then boarded the Peak Tram and as it started its scenic climb we got dizzying glimpses of the island. Finally on reaching the peak and looking down over

The Peak Tram making its journey
to the top of Hong Kong Island.

those high-rise flats on the Island, seeing the harbour and Kowloon on the mainland really was one of the most spectacular, and even exhilarating sights, that I could ever wish to see.

Les and I saw more of Kowloon and Hong Kong Island in those two days than we ever did living there for fourteen months.

On approaching Hong Kong Island by ferry.

134

33

Thanks for the Memories

It was 'Goodbye Hong Kong' as Les and I were once again on yet another troopship, this time the Empire Fowey. We perched ourselves on the rails of the top deck as the ship proceeded so very slowly through the magnificent Victoria Harbour. As we were about to settle down for the long voyage home little did we realise that the sea journey we would be embarking on homewards would take an extra two weeks, extending the journey from four to six weeks before we reached dear old England. This was understandable in view of the circumstances at that particular time, a soldier in the British Army has to accept that sometimes the unaccountable can happen and that is life. None of us knows what is in front of us.

As we sailed from Hong Kong, I was left with mixed feelings but I promised myself that I would one day return and have a holiday there to see those places that I was unable to visit as an Army soldier.

Previously, in Fanling we had been counting the days, fourteen months in Hong Kong, and the excitement of going home had increased dramatically as each day had been ticked off the calendar. We were definitely going home irrespective of whether we enjoyed Hong Kong or not. We came to the assumption there is no place like home but here we were on the Empire Fowey, waving furiously at anyone who was waving to us, and with much good feeling for the place and its people. We waved to the hundreds of boat people as they were called, who lived permanently in their flat bottomed Sampans, which added to the colour and bustle of Victoria Harbour.

This was where some boat people might be lucky and get work in the harbour helping with the loading or unloading of the many ships that arrive in the Victoria Harbour every day. These people really were the poor people of Hong Kong, but nowadays in Hong Kong there may not be so many to be seen.

The excitement seen on the Empire Fowey was very evident as it was not just a few soldiers leaving Hong Kong but the whole of the 2nd Battalion of the Essex Regiment. The Regiment had terminated its time in Hong Kong. After many years there, the Essex Regiment had been assigned to serve in Dortmund, Germany. They would be stationed there for a number of years. After a few weeks leave at home, it would be to Dortmund, that we would have to report for duty and re-join our regiment.

34

The Troopship H.M. Empire Fowey

The Empire Fowey was a turbo-electric ocean liner and she was built in Hamburg, Germany. She was launched in 1935, where she was used as an accommodation ship in Hamburg and then she was ordered to help in the evacuation of East Prussia, as a troopship to Norwegian and Baltic Ports.

It was there that it was seized by the British on the 13th May 1944 at Flensburg and was placed under armed guard by the Royal Navy to prevent the Germans from using her again. It was on route to the USA that war was declared. Within a few weeks the British Armed Guard had to leave Flensburge when a full German Crew re-captured the Empire Fowey when she became involved in the war by sailing around the top of Scotland and the North Sea looking for enemy ships.

At the end of the war she was again used to take families of servicemen to Singapore. In the 1960s she was sold to Pakistan and it was in that country she was scrapped and broken up in a breaking yard there.

So, here we were on the Empire Fowey. This German built troopship of the Second World War. It was an engineering feat of some substance being such a formidable looking sight, as she proceeded on her voyage home to Great Britain. The first port of call would be Singapore where the ship would pick up more British soldiers, who like the Essex Regiment would be returning home. The Empire Fowey was just like our previous ship the Empire Clyde, our sleeping quarters were cabins for five soldiers to share. This arrangement made the sea voyage far more bearable and more convenient in every possible way.

The Troopship H.M. Empire Fowey.

Whereas, The H.M. Dilwara was the first ship we sailed on leaving Southampton. She was built in 1935 and I am sure that all troopships of this era were made the same way. There would be nothing unusual, at that particular time, to the lack of thought for the comfort of its cargo of soldiers. Hopefully troopships are made differently today, fitted with cabins with only five or six soldiers sharing. The last time Great Britain transferred thousands of troops abroad by sea was to retake the Falklands back from Argentina. Here the enemy was also thousands of miles away and I like to think the troops travelled in far superior comfort to us on the Dilwara.

Despite the conditions I endured, it was an amazing experience (although not always pleasant) being on the Dilwara. Surely, just one of these troopships could be put on show somewhere to be a regular reminder to us all of the immense sacrifice made by soldiers in the dark days of the War?

On looking back to the troopship Dilwara, the troop decks were simply appalling places, so much so, that the Empire Fowey gave me the impression we were travelling first class with the excellent food served on the ship. (Take my word for it, we had nothing whatsoever to grumble about.)

"We sleep safely at night because rough men stand ready to visit violence on those who would harm us."

Winston Churchill.

35

Forever Faithful

I cannot recall revisiting Singapore and Ceylon again on the return journey. In all probability there would have been no shore leave when the Empire Fowey would have docked at them. I can only assume the logical explanation was that although the ship did dock at those ports it was for a very short time and certainly not long enough for any shore leave to be given (although I could be wrong).

Some of the Essex boys were definitely getting excited that they would soon be home and with their girlfriends again, for the majority of them it was well over a year since they had seen them and for some it was even longer. I know that all of the Essex boys in some cases had written every day to their girlfriends and just couldn't wait to see them but would all these soldier boys find that happiness which they so desperately needed when they were reunited with their girlfriends once more?

As we get older we can change particularly when that young soldier is sent abroad for that very first time. Returning home after a long time away, he can come home a changed person much to the disappointment of his girlfriend. It can of course work the other way with the girl friend being the changed character, either way it would be interesting the way these situations worked out on seeing that special one once again.

For some it was not a happy ending, but there was the soldier who found his girlfriend had been forever faithful to him and who had waited so patiently for his return because she loved him more than ever. This proved that long separations can work, and hopefully, they lived happily ever after.

36

Closure of the Suez Canal

We were in the Indian Ocean and nearing the Gulf of Aden when we were told about the actions of President Nasser, an Egyptian political leader and President of the United Arab Republic. In April 1954 he was given even more presidential powers by being elected President. His almost immediate action was to begin the nationalization of the Suez Canal and it was closed to international ships. This led to a state of high tension throughout the Middle East and the beginning of the Suez Crisis. This devastating news was so disappointing for all the soldiers on board the Empire Fowey who obviously were looking forward to returning home.

For a couple of days the ship hardly moved as it awaited the outcome of what was going to happen. Much speculation was flying about the Empire Fowey as to what was going to happen and how would we eventually get back to Great Britain. Rumour and counter rumour continued with the possibility of war as the ship was in the vicinity of the Suez Canal with more rumours filtering through two or three times a day. One such rumour speculated that as the Suez Canal was in the vicinity of our ship the 2nd Battalion, The Essex Regiment could be involved in the re-opening the Suez Canal. This would have involved much force and action from our troops but fortunately we were told that nothing had been decided.

President Nasser's reason for closing the Suez Canal really did leave a state of tension in the Middle East. All those ships who would normally use the Canal had no alternative than to set sail to go around the Cape of South Africa causing thousands of extra miles to be travelled. Nasser's aim was to build an Arab Empire stretching across North Africa.

The British and French forces intervened causing widespread differences of opinion in Britain and elsewhere and amid Russian threats, which enabled Nasser to turn a military defeat into a political victory. His success was also helped by Britain's Prime Minister, Anthony Eden's, muddled Middle East Policy. This stress may have been the reason Eden resigning on ill-health grounds, having only been prime minister for eighteen months. In the end the Suez Canal was closed from October 1956-March 1957.

37

Zanzibar

After some time hanging around the stationary Empire Fowey, we learned that the Essex Regiment wouldn't be required to help in any way concerning the Suez Crisis. It was decided that the ship would make its way round the Cape in South Africa. This was the only possible route that the Empire Fowey could favourably take, sailing by the southern ocean, which meant a long voyage for the Empire Fowey. After a few more days in the Indian Ocean our next port of call was a very small island off the East coast of Africa with the name of Zanzibar. Here we were given shore leave for a few hours and the opportunity to explore the island.

Les and I and a couple of the Essex Boys hired a taxi driver to take us around the island and here again were the most luxurious, golden sands imaginable with not one person in sight. I suppose when I was there in 1956, Zanzibar could hardly be called a holiday paradise, but today with the loveliness of such a place with its hot climate, it must be perfect.

The town of Zanzibar was very quiet indeed but what I did notice was the fine buildings that make up the town centre, it was then that I was awoken by the familiar sound of a ball on willow. My instinct told me there was a cricket match somewhere in the vicinity and sure enough behind the town buildings was a cricket match of some importance being played in a field.

There was about three thousand spectators and amid much excitement, as I stood watching and I admit to really missing cricket, and felt a great urge to be involved in this cricket match. For the past couple of years I hadn't played the game and as one with a near fanatical love of cricket, I had really missed it. What I couldn't get over was the size of the crowds and I, for one, never knew that cricket was played in Zanzibar. (Long may it continue.)

A short history of the island of Zanzibar is that it is 30 miles north of Dar Es Salaam and became a Portuguese trading centre in the 16th century. In the 17th Century Zanzibar became a thriving country of the East African Ivory trade and by 1890 was made a British Protectorate together with the neighbouring island of Pemba. These two islands were made an independent country when they eventually joined the mainland known at that time as Tanganyika, which became the Republic of Tanzania. The climate is hot and humid, the average temperature ranges from 19oC (66oF) to 31oC (88oF). The major industries are agriculture and food. The main exports are cotton, coffee, cloves and coconuts. In the 19th Century Zanzibar was used mostly as a base for European explorers and missionaries.

38

The Good, the Bad and the Ugly

South Africa is situated geographically at the southern end of the great African continent and in the year 1956 when we visited Cape Town the country was heavily involved in practicing Apartheid. This meant that the government of South Africa was implicated in racial segregation involving a separate development of racial groups operating throughout the country, where at this particular time South Africa was being ruled by white people only. We had been warned about the apartheid and told not to get involved in any trouble, to walk away if we sensed any trouble.

Having spent a most enjoyable day in Zanzibar, the Empire Fowey set sail the next morning for Cape Town in South Africa, which took four days to arrive. When approaching the Cape we came across extremely choppy seas with high winds making this part of the sea voyage most uncomfortable. We were not prepared for this as most of the return journey to Great Britain we had experienced excellent weather. We did make it to Cape Town where the magnificent

Table Mountain proved to be an unforgettable sight in the background of the city of Cape Town. The Empire Fowey slowly approached the southernmost city in the African continent we were totally unprepared for the crowds of people waiting to greet us on the waterfront waving gleefully. We couldn't understand why, until the ship's Captain speaking on the tannoy, informed all the soldiers that the Empire Fowey was the first British troopship that had called at Cape Town since the Second World War, and this was the reason for such a glorious welcome.

Another reason was that President Nasser shutting down the Suez Canal was front page news all over the world. If we were being turned away by Nasser just the opposite was happening in South Africa. There in Cape Town, families were going overboard in their welcome to the British soldiers. I must admit, because the government of South Africa maintaining white supremacy through apartheid laws. I had not expected such a welcome and generosity in their inviting us into their homes. It was an extraordinary gesture on their part, which was much appreciated. We had a one day's leave and as we disembarked from our ship we found that the good people of Cape Town could be very persuasive inviting British soldiers to spend the day with them. I know many of the soldiers did. It was difficult to refuse such hospitality as their enthusiasm was a joy to behold.

Les and I left our ship and within two minutes two middle aged ladies had asked us if they could show us around the city of Cape Town, which we gladly accepted and after a few hours of sightseeing we were taken to one of their homes. A really good meal had been cooked especially for us. Soon after that, we had our ship to catch. Later that evening as we were to set sail for England but just before leaving Cape Town, on the streets of the city we had our first experience concerning apartheid which was ugly. We witnessed a most unpleasant incident, which was a sharp reminder to Les and I that we were in South Africa and not Great Britain.

We were walking back to the ship, we noticed two young black fifteen year old boys following us, they seemed anxious to talk to us. We stopped and they seemed keen to ask about England. This was the country of South Africa and we had been warned about the apartheid situation throughout the country, we had been told of the hideous laws concerning all black people. Surely I could speak to those two boys if only to ask why were they following us. They asked us, *"What sort of country was England?"*

In the end we were hardly able to speak to them, as a most unpleasant encounter with 'the law', occurred because of this conversation. We heard a white and burly police officer bellowing from across the road, as he started shouting and swearing in our direction that the two young black boys should not be talking to white people. He hurried to get to us, crossed the road, he was very aggressive muttering to himself, and held a whip in his hand. He was a very big fellow and his hatred of the two young black boys was very evident.

The young boys seeing that they were in trouble scarpered out of his sight very quickly. This brute of a policeman told us in no uncertain manner not to speak to black kids as they would soon cause lots of trouble. I was truly dumbfounded by his aggression but he wasn't listening to anything we were saying.

No wonder those two black boys wanted to know what life was like in England after having been born in South Africa.

We had been witness to the good, the bad and the ugly in South Africa. It started with the 'good', being those lovely ladies who had invited us into their homes when we were given as much care and attention, which we would never forget. The 'bad' was seeing Apartheid in action, and the way those two young boys were regarded showed the 'ugly' side. I saw that whip in the policeman's hand, which he would definitely have used on those boys. Also evident that day in Cape Town was the toilets. Writing on the doors stating 'whites only' or 'blacks only'. All this was a wake-up call—I had seen racial segregation and I did not like it.

Cape Town Mountain, South Africa.

39

The Apartheid Policy

Before the Empire Fowey Troopship had docked in Cape Town, we had been warned that the South African Government Apartheid had to be obeyed irrespective of whether we agreed with them or not. We had to be prepared for any distraction that might occur, which had already happened to be the case concerning the two young black boys. We had been told that South Africa could be a very dangerous place for anyone visiting the country.

Les and I were among many soldiers from our ship who would hardly visit Cape Town to cause any trouble. We also had to remember that we were British soldiers in a foreign country and to behave ourselves accordingly. I would have regarded a conversation with those two black boys if only to hear their own life story but the policeman would have none of it.

South Africa's Apartheid Policy in 1956 was, in all probability, the most prominent and decisive issue at that time. As this gruesome and repulsive system which spread across the whole of the Black community, was allowed to operate, where in South Africa one was judged by the colour of one's skin. When I knew instinctively that apartheid was the government policies where the White's ruled the country with vigour, consequently the Black people were treated quite disgracefully and lived in appalling ghettos, which once again reminded me of the mud huts where the very poor lived in Ceylon. I believe this segregation of human beings is horribly and woefully wrong. I also believe, most passionately that everyone in this world should be treated equally regardless of what colour they are.

My Christian faith has always taught me not to discriminate against people of different race and religions, and just to prove that I am not prejudiced in any way, I now list just two of my sporting heroes from years past. One being the boxer, Muhammad Ali who really was the greatest boxer of all time, and Gary Sobers, the greatest West Indies all-rounder at cricket there has ever been.

Basil D'Oliveira, due to the rules of the Apartheid, was unable to play test cricket in South Africa. In 1964, he joined Worcestershire County Cricket Club, England, and within two years made such an impression he was picked to play Test Cricket for England in South Africa (despite his native country being South Africa). His career was full of controversy; South African Prime Minister, B.J. Vorster, remarked D'Oliveira would not be welcomed in South Africa because of his skin colour. As a consequence of this, South Africa was banned from Test Cricket for over 30 years.

40

Plenty of Time for Thought

Once again I had no idea as to what day or date it was when the Empire Fowey sailed from Cape Town on its long voyage before we finally reached England. Later, working out the distance on a world map, I came to the conclusion we must have travelled nearly 6000 miles from Cape Town to Southampton, making it the longest of all the sea journeys during my National Service days. But I have to report that in the Atlantic Ocean it really was for most of the time, *"We're busy doin' nothing, working the whole day through."* Yes, it could really be a lazy life with endless sunbathing.

Having said this, we did keep reasonably busy as everyone was required to do a certain amount of jobs, mine was cleaning out the cabin where five of us, including Les, slept. I have to report that the Empire Fowey would pass any test for cleanliness being as clean as any ship could possibly be.

While lying in the sun most of the day, there was always plenty of time for thought at that particular time and, providing one didn't burn oneself, one could doze off in the sun or begin to speculate what the future might offer. In my case I'd actually completed eighteen months of my two years National Service, with just six months to go. I kept asking myself would I resume my engineering apprenticeship at the Peterborough Power Station when I was demobbed from the army? I knew it made sense to complete that apprenticeship and I also knew my parents would be very disappointed if I didn't complete it, but I had no real love for the job. It had always been an overriding ambition of mine to try an alternative occupation but in some respects, I hadn't much idea of what I wanted to do. What I did want was to be happy and contented in my work, a situation, which I hadn't yet found.

After spending endless hours in the Atlantic Ocean, the Empire Fowey had a port of call on the West African coastline, Free Town in Sierra Leone. After such a long sea voyage, I'm sure every serviceman would have been looking forward to some shore leave wherever this would be, but there was no shore leave available. This really was a huge disappointment to all aboard our ship. Possibly the decision was taken because the ship would only be allowed a few short hours in Freetown, where probably fuel was required, so off we would continue again. We would make Southampton in just over a week and as the time grew closer to arrival at dear old England the excitement was multiplying every mile as the Empire Fowey proceeded on to its final destination.

41

On British Soil Again

We landed on British soil once more at Southampton after cruising through the English Channel. It was, for me, one of the most extraordinary feelings of happiness I had ever encountered in the whole of my young life. I really was as happy as a sand boy playing in the sand. I had come home to the country of my birth. I could now understand why some people, particularly if they had been away from the old Country for some time would want to kiss the ground on taking that first step on English soil again.

For me treading on the sacred ground of England's green and pleasant land was enough as kissing the ground was not an option. I was afraid of making a spectacle of myself, which was the last thing I ever wanted to do. I may have been accused of showing off, but it was a tempting thought. Surely though, if I had taken the bull by the horns, so to speak, it would have been acceptable that just one soldier in Her Majesty's Service should have been allowed to kiss the ground of the country that he loved so much irrespective whether he would have been allowed to or not.

So there we were. Les and I stood watching the proceedings from the top deck of the Empire Fowey troopship. The disembarkation had already begun and evidently it would be many hours before the Essex Regiment would be allowed to leave with all the luggage. Kit bags carrying all our army clothes and a packed suitcase, which included one's, own personal civilian clothes and even another small suitcase, which included many presents, for loved ones bought in Fanling. What was most notable from our view point, we had an excellent position, with soldiers and their girlfriends running into each other's arms. Mums and dads were not missing out either, lovingly greeting their sons amid much joy and happiness, and my turn to see loved ones would come the next day. The very next morning Les and I would be travelling on different trains, and I would see him during my three weeks. I would visit Les at his home in order to meet his parents, and his girlfriend Yvonne, over a weekend.

42

Welcome Home

On the train to Peterborough were several of the lads who like me had been transferred from the Northamptonshire Regiment to the Essex Regiment. Two were the soldiers I had travelled by train with, that very first day on joining the army at Northampton. I never actually saw much of them in Hong Kong as we were in a different Company, but it is fair to say that whenever I was to see them in the future, Hong Kong would always be the main topic of conversation and never forgotten.

On approaching Peterborough, my excitement was increasing alarmingly. As the train passed Peterborough Power Station where I'd been serving my apprenticeship, I was sure that my life since I had joined the army had been more worthwhile by serving my country than if I'd still been working at the Power Station. The old place looked exactly the same as nothing had changed, but I knew I had. My parents all along knew that the second battalion the Essex Regiment would soon be leaving Hong Kong and I'd told them by letter that I hoped to be home in early September 1956. Going round the Cape it meant that a further two weeks had been added to the voyage making it six weeks on the Empire Fowey from when we left Hong Kong. I arrived at Peterborough North Station I was once again in my home city with a kit bag and heavy suitcase to carry. I had decided to go home in style by ordering a taxi to take me to Church Street in Stanground, where I was born, which fortunately hadn't altered one bit. Walking round the back of the house I found my father in the conservatory. Now, my Dad was quite a reserved person, there would be no greetings with our arms around each other—that was not his style. His handshake was warm and comfortable and that said it all. Then I saw my mother who had tears in her eyes which was so understandable as I knew she would have worried about me more than anyone. We hugged each other very joyfully. A mother's love is so important to a young teenage soldier serving abroad who had never left home before. He would look forward to receiving his mother's letters knowing full well the mother would never send her son a 'Dear John' letter.

During home leave it was a case of once again visiting relatives and friends. Visiting these people didn't mean just for a few minutes, sometimes it was actually a few hours, which really did take up a lot of my time. What I did find was that a lot of my old friends had been called up themselves for National Service or that they were on an apprenticeship somewhere. So I was unable to see them.

During that home leave I'd have a drink with my father and brothers at the local pubs in Stanground. I'm sure my father was a very proud man to be seen with his sons. My mother, however, was quite a religious lady who refrained forever from going into a pub in Stanground, much preferring to attend the local parish church every Sunday. I'm sure that the three weeks home leave that I had been given actually went very quickly indeed.

"Live for something rather than die for nothing."

George Patton.

43

Wise Words Indeed

During my home leave I had been invited to spend a few days with my friend, Les, at his family home in Raunds, Northamptonshire. I met Les' parents and his girlfriend, Yvonne. I had agreed to be Les' best man at the forthcoming wedding, planned for early 1957. I enjoyed meeting them all and joining up with Les once again. Les seemed determined to make it a grand occasion. He couldn't wait for the opportunity to take me to his favourite pub known as the Woodbine Club in Raunds. It quickly became apparent that Les was extremely popular in this club, and seemed to know everyone there, and because of this there was plenty of alcohol flying about. I knew from my friendship with Les that this was the ideal opportunity for him to indulge in a glass of beer or two (or maybe three or four).

He like everyone else just wouldn't have had sufficient money in Hong Kong to spend on drink. I refrained on some of the drink being offered to me but Les was enjoying himself to the utmost. I would always settle for a couple of pints and remained sober, this being my preference wherever I might be. I will now once more delve into my memory again and try to remember what Les told me that day.

At the Woodbine Club, Les said, *"Brian, when we were on the front line near the communist border overlooking China. I would often think of the Woodbine Club and wonder if I'd ever set eyes on this place again."*

We well knew there was always the fear that China's troops would one day cross over the border and invade Hong Kong. I was at times fearful that the small contingent of British Forces in Hong Kong would offer little resistance by being massively outnumbered by thousands of China's Troops who could have overwhelmed us completely. We would not be sitting here if that had happened.

Les continued, *"Today we have much to be happy about and this is a day I wish to celebrate with you here in the Woodbine Club, being the place I used to dream about."*

I had to agree with Les as that was exactly how I felt, but with me it was my family who I always thought about during such stressful times and of course the green fields of England. Les had put everything in its proper perspective on judging the relative importance of such an occasion where his words were wise indeed.

44

Germany

In next to no time, I was getting ready to return to the Army at the end of October and I wasn't sure whether I would be home for Christmas. If not, the next likely date would be when I was demobbed in February the following year, when my two years National Service would have been completed. I had a few months to see out my National Service and was on the move again, my next posting was to be Dortmund in West Germany.

So, the Essex soldiers began to prepare for moving to Germany. At a rough guess it would be late October 1956 when soldiers of the 2nd Battalion the Essex Regiment were notified to report to Kings Cross Railway Station in London. We had to prepare for the short sea voyage, crossing over the North Sea from Harwich to the Hook-of-Holland. This short sea voyage between Great Britain and Holland turned out to be the roughest of all seas imaginable.

All those small troopships took a hell of a battering and seemed totally unsuited for the gale force winds we met that night.

What was remembered that night was the thousands of miles we had previously undertaken by sailing halfway across the world to Hong Kong and back. We barely met any rough seas, apart from the Bay of Biscay, and sailing around the cape in South Africa, but the North Sea could be frightening and I've never seen so many soldiers all ill at the same time.

It was at the sea port of the Hook-of-Holland when I met up with scores of Essex soldiers who like myself were making for Germany. I really relished being in their company, but for the life of me since those army days of over sixty years ago I have now forgotten many of their names. I have many photographs of them and that's all I have but I have to admit that with creaking old age my memory although it is still good, is not what it was. It was at the Hook-of-Holland that transportation in the form of lorries that we were taken the one hundred or so miles to Dortmund whereby those lorries with their hard seats were the cause of many sore backsides. At Dortmund, our barracks were shared with other regiments and we were left with the feelings that the barrack rooms were not entirely ours.

Of course, after the end of the Second World War Germany had been divided into the two Germanys. East Germany which had electrical fences and minefields installed to keep intruders out and others in.

Russian domination controlled everything in East Germany. Yet West Germany since the end of the Second World War had achieved incredible accomplishments by rebuilding.

This was the situation in Germany when I was there in 1956. I was stationed there where British regiments along with other country's regiments were sent to keep the peace. There was a possibility that with, Russian influence, Germany could fall but it never happened and some thirty years later Germany became its own country once again. I was only in Germany for a few short months in comparison to the fourteen months I spent in Hong Kong (which had left me with many treasured memories).

I never really settled in Germany, I believe that the German people never quite appreciated us being there and I can remember some British soldiers retaliating after being set upon by Germans in the streets of Dortmund.

I can also remember an Essex soldier, Sergeant Joe Richardson, ordering us Essex soldiers out of a pub because German teenagers were trying to cause much trouble inside the pub, which probably saved an ugly confrontation from ever happening. The relationship with German people was nowhere near as good as it was with the people of Hong Kong, where the locals, in particular, the shopkeepers in Fanling, were real gentlemen. We the British soldiers were always made welcome wherever we were in Hong Kong. Of course the weather with all its sunshine in Hong Kong helped enormously.

The weather in Germany at that time was bitterly cold with snow at times, which I very much resented and after the sunshine of Hong Kong I for one always felt the cold. Fortunately, I was able to play plenty of football for the B Company Football team. There was an excellent NAAFI on the camp where we spent a considerable amount of time. The work we had to do was very similar to the work we did in Hong Kong with plenty of square bashing, so nothing really changed, but I have to be honest that I much preferred to be a soldier in Hong Kong than in West Germany.

My best pal, Les.
We were being split up when on leaving Les,
he placed in my hand a photograph of himself
which I put in my kitbag. Years later I came
across this photograph Les had given me. On
turning over the photo Les had written,
"Just something to remember me by".
It was enough to make me weep.

45

"I'll see you at the Wedding"

Les couldn't believe it or should I write, he blatantly refused to believe it. He was up-in-arms over it! The cause of such an upset was that we were to be parted for the last four weeks of our time together in the Army. I, for some unknown reason, had been picked to attend a First Aid course in Epsom in Surrey. I hardly looked forward to such a move. I wanted to be with Les and those Essex boys who had really been a part of my two years in the Essex Regiment. Les and I had really enjoyed our last Christmas in 1956 together with demob being just six weeks away.

I'd never seen Les in such a state of uncontrolled grievance. He really was very upset, "It can't be" he said "I'm really going to get stuck into our Platoon Officer when I see him." I was equally upset over what had happened, and the rumpus it was causing really was a noisy commotion. When Les got annoyed, a vocabulary of many different choice words would often be expressed and this was one such occasion. It was in the 1st week of January 1957 when I was notified that I'd be attending the First Aid course. Les and I had tried our utmost to stay together. Les had actually asked our Platoon Officer if he could also attend this course and I made it known that I wasn't going anywhere! However, my pleading was to no avail. Les rumbled on.

"I've travelled the world for nearly two years with you Brian, and we have chalked up literally thousands of miles together, but now some idiot in some army office somewhere is trying to split us up."

I could well understand his feelings as mine were exactly the same. Our last night with our last pint of beer in the NAAFI was hardly exciting and there was nothing to cheer us up. I was saying cheerio to most of the Essex boys and this goodbye was as dead as a doormat. It should have been a happy occasion, which we had intended it to be, but not anymore. The next morning, I was up especially early as I had a train to catch to the Hook-of-Holland. I could see my best pal, Les, was still upset and as we shook hands. I managed to stammer, *"I'll see you at the wedding"*, and I was gone. The wedding date had been brought forward by a few months because of natural circumstances.

Regards the First Aid course, I did try to enjoy this course but it felt as though something was missing in my life and it was my best friend. I was sure Les was experiencing much the same, because when we were together we were a good combination. I am sure we would have gone through a brick wall for each other and it's uncanny that we managed to stay together for nearly two years, apart from the last four weeks. Friendships made in the Forces stand the test of time and ours most definitely did.

46

The End of My National Service

National Service was brought in just after the Second World War when it became compulsory for every young man at eighteen years of age throughout Great Britain to sign on. The only ones exempt from the call-up were those who were unable to partake in the Army, Navy or the Royal Air Force due to health reasons. I do believe National Service in my time really was part of a young man's development and to a certain extent his education and that he was the better for such an episode in his young life. At home with his mother he would never have made his bed or ironed a shirt and probably never leave the family home.

In all honesty I can state that at times I enjoyed National Service but at other times I may have disliked the daily drudge of it, the continued wearisome way of everyday life. I am reminded on looking back that the good part of army life certainly outweighed all the bad parts and that made the very existence of being in the army more than just bearable. One thing that I enjoyed in the army without fail was the sports I was involved with, it always brought much satisfaction, and if one did play sports in the army one definitely had a better life of it and were often excused some of the more arduous duties of army life.

It was very special when a soldier returns home after nearly two years abroad to finally resume his courtship with his long standing girlfriend where both have been loyal to each other. As they run into each other's arms and although they were openly expressing much love to each other which was lovely to see, but I didn't necessarily want that kind of relationship. I was only twenty-one years of age at the time so I preferred to stay single. As my father would say, *"There's plenty of fish on the pond."* As I hope marriage was some distance away I wanted a secure job first and to indulge in the sports I played.

My mother didn't encourage any of her sons into an early marriage. This was good advice as all her sons were married in their late twenties. My mother worried herself considerably when I was in Hong Kong that I would arrive home with a Chinese girlfriend who was heavily pregnant. Fortunately, it never happened, much to my mother's relief. How on earth could I have let my mother down I ask you?

I do believe that being away from home in my two years of serving my country was the making of me where being in the army made me more independent and definitely more confident. My mother immediately noticed the change in me, because on leaving home to go abroad I was a young boy who in some respects had a lot to learn and didn't always know the ways of the world. She recognised the necessary change in her son. However, my two years National Service had changed all that. I have heard it said, that when an eighteen year old boy goes into the Forces he comes out after two years, a man. I can vouch for that.

I must mention my old friend Les Knight for the last time, because if it wasn't for National Service we would never have met and yes, I did go to his wedding where I performed the duties of Best Man. I can confirm it was a really happy occasion. Soon after however, they began to have problems and eventually Les and Yvonne split up.

I have to report that Les did marry for a second time to Gil on 26 October 1963 and the marriage produced two boys and a girl and was a happy marriage. I was so pleased that my old army buddy had found true happiness, he deserved it.

I have already mentioned in this book that Les died a few years ago (December 2006) and since I have been writing about the earlier part of my life in the Army it has meant that Les has never been far away from my thoughts, inevitably, considering the amount of time we were together. As I write, I have a very strange feeling that Les is in my presence. Sometimes, this is so apparent that when I hand write on an A4 refill pad if I'm not entirely pleased with what I've written, I will then tear out that page and start again with the hope I will have his approval.

—⟨ᴓᴓᴓ⟩—

*"The highest of distinctions is
service to others."*

King George VI.

—⟨ᴓᴓᴓ⟩—

47

A Happy Demob Day

Demob Day was a happy day, which I celebrated at Epsom in Surrey on the 10th February in 1957. When I had finished the First Aid course, along with other soldiers from other regiments, we actually celebrated in the proper manner by drinking numerous cups of tea, with nothing stronger. So here I was, with all the others as we reminisced about our two years National Service, with many tales to tell where I just about tolerated army life but I was never to fall in love with it. I must emphasize that I certainly would never have missed what I saw, but came to realise that some of the soldiers that day had spent the whole of their two years' National Service in Great Britain. When I mentioned the countries I had seen in my two years they looked quite envious and remarked how fortunate I had been.

From this day onwards there would be: no square bashing; no more spit and polish on cleaning the Army boots; no more kit inspections; no more peeling spuds; no more running up hills in full battledress; no more digging trenches, and the countless other tasks I had been required to do. There was one thing I would really miss, and that would be the camaraderie I had found in the barrack room in B Company of the Essex Regiment, where at times it was incredibly hilarious. I'm sure that this camaraderie could apply to all barrack rooms that were home to the British Army lads. It was a very infectious type of humour, most of our barrack rooms had a comedian, who it has to be said were worth their weight in gold in keeping all our spirits up.

The only real criticism I can possibly make concerning my two years as a National Service soldier was the shortage of a decent wage, and in many respects it stopped soldiers, myself included from visiting other areas. In particular Hong Kong was a place I would love to have seen much more. This has been an undoubted regret going back over sixty years, my expectations of Hong Kong where I had visualised all sorts of interesting escapades to enjoy myself, but that never materialised. Consequently a pint of beer and a cigarette most evenings in the NAAFI was indeed our only luxury. Yes, we could afford that but any notion that I had of exploring Hong Kong and its surrounding areas was quickly squashed, as money was short. I still believe Hong Kong was one of the best postings in the British Army during that time.

I am sure that it was not too irregular that I served my two years National Service with two different infantry regiments. The 1st Battalion of the Northamptonshire Regiment where I did my initial Army training at Quebec Barracks, Northampton and the 2nd Battalion of the Essex Regiment. This had happened when the Essex Regiment required more soldiers at that particular time, because they were under strength while serving in Hong Kong. A transfer took place involving nearly all the soldiers who had taken part in the passing out parade at Quebec Barracks in April 1955.

Concerning both of these fine regiments: If I had the choice of serving in either of these regiments then I must refrain from being Judge and Jury! I was sure I'd find it very difficult indeed to favour one such regiment above the other. I mentioned earlier in this book that I hoped my time in Hong Kong would not be a disappointment for me, in view of the fact, that I was hell bent on seeing Hong Kong. I know the very first sight of seeing Hong Kong can take one's breath away. Sailing into the magnificent Victoria Harbour is a truly glorious sight and I speak for all the Essex boys as we saw that first glimpse of the country. To see the sky high flats on Hong Kong Island and the city of Kowloon on the mainland – it gave the whole place a vibrant atmosphere amongst a most spectacular setting.

Page 1

Army Book 111

№ 708058

Surname and Initials

Army No.

Group No.

Discharge from Whole-Time
and
Entry upon Part-Time Military Service
of a National Service Soldier

Any person finding this book is requested to hand it in to any Barracks, Post Office or Police Station, for transmission to the Under-Secretary of State, The War Office, London, S.W.1

Designation of HQ, AER or TA Unit to which the soldier will report

Date due to report

B W Holdich 29115506

MILITARY CONDUCT. *Very good*

NOTE—The Range of Military Conduct Gradings possible is :—
(1) Very Good (2) Good (3) Fair (4) Indifferent (5) Bad (6) Very Bad

Page 10
Army
Book
111

Testimonial. (To be completed with a view to civil employment and to be identical with that on page 8.)

Comment reads:
L/C Holdich is a pleasant man and is thoroughly trustworthy. He has shown some leadership in his work and he has always been smart and well turned out.

Discharge Paper

48

A Civilian Again

On leaving the British Army I returned to Great
Britain to complete my apprenticeship at the
Peterborough Power Station, where eventually I
became very despondent within myself and I felt I
must try something different in my work. I could
only settle for short periods in other jobs and also
living at home with my mother and father again.
My mother couldn't understand why I wanted to
socialise every evening somewhere. Could it be that
I was missing the Army? 'Surely not!' I thought, but
if I was it was perfectly genuine, in view of all the
travelling I had done during those two years in the
Army, I was becoming restless.

At that time I would invariably think about how
the other soldiers, who had been demobbed, like me.
How were they coping in civilian life? For some life
would never be easy after serving their two years
of National Service, but I really did have a stroke
of good fortune when I joined the Prudential and
became 'The Man from the Pru'.

Almost immediately I seemed to have found what I had been looking for. It is where I was employed for 30 years as an insurance agent, which suited my personality. There, I found my employment utopia, as I couldn't have been happier selling insurance to clients and dealing with claims etc.

On coming to the end of my story concerning two years of National Service and unfortunately there is no such thing today and I don't suppose it will ever return. That is of course a good thing because if it ever did return Great Britain could be involved in a Third World War and God help us in that situation. However, National Service did have a purpose at that particular time and writing this story has brought back memories galore. My father once said to me, *"The Army has made a man of you, my boy."* Of course he was so right. National Service was my salvation and before I joined the Army I was going nowhere. The Army rescued me from adversity and life could only get better. For me it was character building.

49

No Regrets

My biggest ambition by far in the army was to visit as many countries as possible and I certainly achieved that. Just imagine how much it would cost with all the travelling I undertook, to see parts of the world. Undoubtedly, it would have cost many thousands of pounds. At my time of life I really appreciated what I saw and fortunately not all has been forgotten. Since I've been writing this book I have spoken to many ex National Servicemen and they virtually all agreed they wouldn't have missed such an experience. Some even remarked that National Service ought to be brought back if only to put some discipline into some of today's youngsters lives. National Service gradually finished in the early sixties and I can't see it returning. I know that I am still grateful for it and the two years I completed I can remember far more than any other two years of my entire life. Surely, this means something very special!

What is quite extraordinary writing about days well and truly past is my memory continues to surprise me with what I have remembered. It's been really special and I have no regrets at all concerning my two years of National Service, which hopefully one could have gathered that on reading this book. It has been a pleasure with the help of my neighbour and the Collins Atlas Book of the World, to set about finding how many miles I had completed along with fellow soldiers of the Essex Regiment. As we sailed on the many seas of the world going back over sixty years, when I sailed from Southampton to Hong Kong, and then returned on a diverted sea voyage.

In my two years of National Service I had visited Aden, Ceylon, Singapore, Hong Kong, Zanzibar, South Africa, Holland and Germany and I sailed on the three troopships; the Dilwara, The Empire Clyde, and the Empire Fowey. I had sailed on some of the great seas of the world. The total number of miles travelled was over twenty eight thousand miles. I have always thought how fortunate I have been to see so much of the world, when I was just a teenager but being much older now I consider it to be my journey of a lifetime. I wouldn't change anything (apart from jankers of course). Whoever said National Service was boring?

50

Never Forgotten

On having served most of my National Service in Hong Kong. I have never forgotten that most beautiful part of the world with the city of Kowloon being the type of city one would never tire of. Kowloon is a place where everyone who's ever been there would wish to visit it again and again, with myself being no exception. So it really was my desire, that one day with my wife Kathleen and I would visit there again with more money in my pocket, than in my army days and to really enjoy a wonderful holiday there. Unfortunately, this trip never did materialise and I never did get the opportunity to revisit Hong Kong. I always thought, particularly when I retired from work, I would have sufficient time to travel once more to the Far East.

As the years swiftly went by, both Kathleen and I began to have health problems, which certainly restricted us from visiting anywhere abroad, but it would have been fascinating to have seen all the changes that have taken place there and I was so disappointed that I wouldn't be returning to Hong

Kong again. I'm sure we can all learn from mistakes made in our lives. So my advice therefore is, that if one is thinking of taking an overseas holiday abroad, then take it before one gets too old as you never know what is in front of us.

In the revised edition I can now confirm that communist China are in the process of changing the Hong Kong I knew as a serving British soldier.

In 2022, it will be the 25-year anniversary of the British handover back to China their legal control of Hong Kong. In its heyday, Hong Kong was one of the most successful economic countries in the Western World. This small British colony became a showcase for Capitalism, stability and prosperity producing many exceptional business empires.

Boris Johnson, during his time as British Foreign Secretary, expressed a hope that the People's Republic of China would continue progress in keeping Hong Kong democratic and accountable in governance. Instability has already been created and Hong Kong residents put under intense pressure; freedom of speech greatly affected; large companies are being investigated and assets being frozen; arrests on trumped up charges and imprisonment related to these charges. Today's Hong Kong does not seem, to me, a very pleasant place to be. Younger Hong Kong citizens have bravely protested on the streets about the harshness of new laws.

I am worried about the future of Hong Kong: in my mind a place of beauty which left me always wanting to see more. During my service, Hong Kong was always regarded as the Jewel in the Crown by British troops there, I'm not sure whether it still applies today.

Epilogue

If any young person reading this book is interested in joining the Army and making it a career, it could be exactly what you are looking for. Many young people at eighteen in Great Britain today are unemployed, having unsuccessfully been able to find work and as a result become depressed at the hopelessness they find themselves in. What could be better for any young person, who is thinking of joining the Army? Where at the very least the prospect of promotion is very good with a weekly wage evidently far better than any money they might receive when permanently on the dole. It could be the opportunity you are looking for. For no one fully understands a job unless they try it themselves.

The British Army will always want soldiers, providing them with the opportunity of travel and plenty of sport and leisure opportunities. What would be the better option between being out of work for a long period of time or serving your country in the Armed Forces? The choice is yours.

I would like the reader to understand that it would be virtually impossible to remember everything that occurred in those two years as a National Service soldier, and I believe this narrative is as near to the

'B' Company of the 2nd Battalion of the Essex Regiment - Fanling Army Camp 1956
The author is standing second row, fifth from the left.

truth as I could possibly get and if I have made any errors I humbly apologise. If this book is read by ex soldiers of the Northamptonshire Regiment and the Essex Regiment I hope they remember me (1955-1957) and can clarify what I have written is the truth. Surely, I couldn't make up a story of such magnitude could I? And going back over 60 years I am so grateful that I have managed to put my story into print before one gets any older and all is then lost forever.

I have a photograph of B Company of the Essex Regiment taken at the Fanling Army Camp in 1956, where 80 soldiers are smiling for the camera. This photograph is hanging from the wall in my office at home where I'm constantly reminded of what a good set of soldiers they were who made life very much more bearable. Nearly all these soldiers are young men, with their lives in front of them. Where in all probability I would see them every day, and many would be good friends, but now I can only pick out six names from the eighty, which makes me feel rather sad. It could be that we would now pass each other in the street, somewhere but because we would have altered quite substantively, we would not recognise each other anymore. I suppose going back over sixty years is understandable.

What is evermore sad is that some of those soldiers have passed on to that great Christian Regiment in the sky where we all hope to meet up again one day.

For me, they seem to have vanished into thin air as we realise the years have passed us by. We hadn't heard a passing comment about them so now it's time to let them go, by saying goodbye which nearly brings a tear to my eye.

I have only one disappointment concerning my time in Hong Kong. In 1939 the Second World War was about to start and 5,000 youngsters known as evacuees arrived in Peterborough and would live with Peterborough families. This occurred as it was known that London would be bombed by German aircraft and to protect those evacuees by moving them to less populated areas in Britain. My parents had volunteered to have a young boy, Derek aged 7 years old, I was 5 years old, and we became great friends. When the war was over, Derek and I kept in touch spasmodically, once there was a gap of over 20 years between speaking. When we did get in touch we had lots to tell each other and this was when National Service was mentioned and we found out we were both in Hong Kong at the same time (1955-1957) Derek was in the RAF and myself a soldier. On working out the distance separating each other, it was just five miles. What a coincidence, but it would have been even better if we had been able to meet in Hong Kong. I would have loved to have seen him as we would have lots to talk about. Strange what life can throw up when it's least expected.

Ingram Content Group UK Ltd.
Milton Keynes UK
UKHW021948100323
418399UK00009B/127